Knit Couture

Knit Couture

20 Hand-knit Designs from Runway to Reality

Gail Downey & Henry Conway

St. Martin's Press
New York

The authors would like to dedicate the book to Derek Downey and Nan Lamb for their inspiration.

www.stmartins.com

Library of Congress Cataloging-in-Publication Data Available Upon Request

First published in Great Britain by Collins & Brown

First U.S. Edition: January 2008

10 9 8 7 6 5 4 3 2 1

ISBN-13: 978-0-312-37580-5
ISBN-10: 0-312-37580-8

Commissioning Editor: Michelle Lo
Design Manager: Gemma Wilson
Editor: Kate Haxell
Designer: Abby Franklin
Photographers: Richard Stow (pages 2,4,6, 8, 11, 12, 13, 14, 15, 17, 38, 41, 131, 133) and Roger Dean (pages 130-133))
Hand Illustrations: Nicole Heidaripour
Technical Illustrator: Luise Roberts
Picture Researchers: Emily Hedges & David Penrose
Senior Production Controller: Morna McPherson

Reproduction by Spectrum Colour Ltd, UK
Printed and bound by SNP Leefung, China

The publishers would like to thank the following sources for their kind permission to reproduce the photographs and illustrations in this book.

Key
BAL = Bridgeman Art Library
V&A = V&A Images/Victoria and Albert Museum

19 Aberdeen Art Gallery & Museums Collections, 21 & 22 V&A, 23 Hamburger Kunsthalle, Hamburg/BAL, 24 NTPL/John Hammond, 25 V&A, 26 Royal Institution of Cornwall (POPgv030), 27 Archives Larousse, Paris/Giraudon/BAL, 28 Musee de la Ville de Paris, Musee Carnavalet, Paris/Lauros/Giraudon/BAL, 29 NMPFT/Daily Herald Archive, 30 Getty Images, 33 Philadelphia Museum of Art/Corbis, 34 Bettmann/Corbis, 37 Woolcraft, 43 Vauthey Pierre/Corbix Sygma, 44 Alfred/epa/Corbis, 47 Orban Thierry/Corbis Sygma, 48 Charles Platiau/Reuters/Corbis, 49 Tanguy Loyzance/Corbis, 51 Orban Thierry/Corbis Sygma, 52 Richard Young/Rex Features, 54 Paramont/The Kobal Collection, 57 Marion Foale, 59 Bettmann/Corbis, 66 Rune Hellestad/Corbis, 67 Pringle of Scotland Spring Summer 2007 advertising campaign, 68 Dygo Sasaki/Lowie

"We would like to thank Amy Wear, Roger Dean, Rose Ward, Peter Middleton, Derek and Colette Conway, The Cockpit Theatre, Ed at ICM Model Management, Eileen Lawrence, all at Weardowney, Marie at Rowan Yarns, Charlotte Weston, Sophia Dawney and our army of silent helpers."

78

118

88

116

114

Contents

Introduction

Hand knitting has been somewhat neglected by fashion history. Indeed, only recently has knitwear in general been given any considerable attention. This is partly due to the organic nature of handcraftsmanship—in looking at the development of hand knitwear and its place today, one sees that it is a deceptively large area of study. Hand knitting is a quiet part of many cultures all over the world, having been developed in subtly different ways for centuries. From the small community-based knits of the East Coast of the USA, to the practical patterns of Scandinavia, to the application of hand knit in high fashion, hand knitwear makes up part of many ever-evolving cultural landscapes.

Hand knitting's organic nature makes it ever stronger, as it evolves and changes on an individual level. Each shift in approach is not only a reflection of the culture from which it was born but also a reflection of the environment of the protagonist, with an individual's practical and aesthetic vision realized in a physical form: simple, tempered, methodical knitting. With its practicability, decorative potential, and the unhurried pace at which it must be executed, hand knitting must be fashion's most charming medium.

Over the past few years an increased interest in hand knitting has resulted in an international rediscovery of the medium. The craft's momentum has now built to the point where we can see knitting truly emerge as a movement in itself.

Being a medium that is self-absorbing without being self-obsessed, the reemergence of hand knitting has caused a revival in directional knitwear. There is a culpable sense that this movement is driving knit forward into previously untested areas and we can see the revival in terms of a new versatility in the medium. Indeed, throughout the centuries knitwear has pushed on, both technically and aesthetically, as it is

essentially a mimic. In copying other textiles and forms, knit has often brought an entirely different light and purpose to the original material.

As its methods are translated to suit machine knitting, the techniques of hand knitting are now mimicked and applied to other functions. Knit can afford to be fluid, to explore its sculptural, dynamic, and morphic qualities. The legendary couturier Elsa Schiaparelli started in knitwear and exploited these qualities, setting the standards for knit in modern fashion. From Aran to chunky cable knits, the medium and industry have been pushed forward in fashion by the technical and aesthetic versatility of hand knitwear. With knits seen in swimwear, sportswear, accessories and in nightclubs, the medium is now more versatile than ever before.

Along with charting the development of hand knitting from its origins to its introduction into the lexicon of fashion, *Knit Couture* will profile the key protagonists of hand knit and knit in the last half of the twentieth century, as well as those who are most important as we progress into the twenty-first—the next generation moving the medium on.

It is not just in fashion that hand knitting is making an impression. Properties of the medium are being translated into industrial and non-garment textiles. From the application of knit to architecture, to geo-textiles and medical textiles, knit is at the heart of progressive technology.

Both at an industrial and an individual level, hand knitting is moving knitwear into new areas previously unimagined. From garments to the linings of aircraft, hand knitting is a quiet but powerful force. We hope that *Knit Couture* will inspire, instruct and give insight into the charming and infinite craft of hand knitting.

Gail Downey and Henry Conway, 2007

Weardowney

For the London-based hand knitwear label Weardowney, knitting is a way of life. Amy Wear, a former catwalk model, and Gail Downey, knitwear designer for John Galliano for six years in the 1980s and also a former model, formed the label in 2004. Weardowney is much more than simply a label; it has grown into the "House of Weardowney" with multiple facets—a truly "composite business." Emanating from its boutique in Marylebone, London, it now encompasses a diffusion line for Topshop, a cosmopolitan guesthouse, a school of handcraftsmanship and a biannual magazine.

The company's approach has been described as a "gloss on the artisan," and the ethos of Weardowney is the antithesis of a regular contemporary fashion label. It is devoted to the advancement of the craft of knitting and, through this, the advancement of craft itself. The emphasis in all that Weardowney dedicates itself to is on consciously striving to propagate the continuation and advancement of handcraftsmanship—the idea that making things with the hands is intelligent, tempered, worthwhile, and, to some people, even therapeutic. They believe that hand, heart, and mind all combine in handcraftsmanship, and indeed Weardowney has adopted a quote from Fritz Lang's 1927 film *Metropolis* to sum up its entire approach: "There can be no understanding between the hands and the brain unless the heart acts as mediator."

The Get Up boutique in Marylebone is the backdrop to the House of Weardowney. The former pub has been converted into an airy boutique that sells the Weardowney hand knits, knitting kits, and

to learn the craft. Four million women in the UK have an interest in knitting and an estimated 475,000 people took it up in the UK and USA in 2006.[1] This quiet craft is beginning to make some noise. Weardowney now also produces knitting kits, presented in vintage-inspired half-hatboxes, that come with everything you need to make Weardowney pieces. The skill levels are in four categories—Beginner, Facile, Fiddly, and Fiendish.

Weardowney has also expanded from fashions creations to a fashion publication. The *WD* biannual magazine has been a success, with the last two issues distributed to boutiques, hotels, salons, and other outlets not only in London and the UK, but all over the world: the magazine counts some of the top movers in fashion among its readership. Taking the ethos of Weardowney and translating it into a magazine was a natural process. Spring/Summer 2006's *Passion and Craftsmanship* and Autumn/Winter 2006/7's *The Honourable Tradesman* both contained articles on art, historic costume, film, and drama, and of course fashion, with a focus on the *craft* of these subjects.

The clothes collections themselves are a testament to Weardowney's commitment to moving knit forward. The company strives to be a technical innovator in the medium of hand knitting, alongside progressing their aesthetic. Their signature yarn is lurex—the subtle shimmer enhances the form-fitting shapes that the knit creates, and the drape and handle are elegant, not spongy, in texture.

This consideration of the body is key to Weardowney's design ethos of using the natural property of knit as a fabric to mold around the body. To do this they concentrate on the qualities of knit from a hand knitting point of view. Where some designers treat knitted fabric in the same way as any other textiles—cutting and panelling it flat to form a garment's shape—Weardowney uses the process of knitting to move their designs

a variety of other labels and items that reflect the company's values. Contemporary clothes from Jean Pierre Braganza sit alongside worked-metal and crystal Cesar Perin chandeliers and Shaker-style clothes pegs, creating a modern vintage look. Legendary Parisian designer Loulou de la Falaise, Yves Saint Laurent's jewelry and accessories designer and his muse for thirty years, now sells her own line of gorgeous jewelry exclusively through the boutique.

Based at the boutique is the Weardowney School of Handcraftsmanship. This developed out of an increasing demand for knitting education. The classes have revealed the extraordinary diversity of those interested in knitting. Hedge fund managers sit alongside public relations directors

---

1. Statistics from www.bhkc.co.uk

forward: the shape is created by knitting patterns, rather than constructing a garment from pre-knitted panels.

An example of this is the Target Shrug, one of the label's first commercial successes. The shrug uses circular knitting, working outward in a radiant that can be altered (at pattern stage) to be octagonal or pentagonal. This pattern is one of Weardowney's most enduringly popular, as it shapes into the body at the back, creating a tight silhouette while being relaxed at the front. It also demonstrates the advantage of building a garment by knitting. The garment is designed in three dimensions rather than flat—both the design and making stages happening concurrently—leading to more effective shaping. The introduction of circular knitting was copied by many other companies and is now featured heavily both on the catwalks and in mainstream stores.

Weardowney does not just create innovative garments, it has led the field in knitted accessories as well. A collaboration for the 2005 Eden collection with Thornton's, the confectioner, led to a range of knitted bags in the shapes of sweets. Knitted headdresses created with Weardowney and Erickson Beamon are beautiful pieces of fantasy in knit. They comprise "head armor" with a Spartan feel, built up with knitted flowers and greenery mounted on wire and rope. Weardowney will also be launching a range of luggage combining knit and painted leather. However, the most innovative of its non-garment collaborations are the sock boots, produced with London shoemaker Jenne O. These are made from circular knitting and use knit's ability to mimic shape in creating a boot that is fully fitted to the leg. They can be worn pulled up to the knee or rolled down to become an ankle boot.

More than anything, Weardowney is passionate about community, and indeed the clothes would not be made if it were not for the community of knitters the company has built up. The ready-to-

wear collection is made in-house and by skilled hand knitters and their apprentices all over the UK. They execute, and pass on, their extraordinary skills in time-honored tradition. Each hand knitter brings their own unique character to the garment and, not being pressured by time, their love of knitting shows through as much as their technical skill. By way of example, one of the Weardowney knitters, Rose Ward, showed her skill in a sample that was created from a pattern for *Elle* magazine. When the editor received the sample she couldn't believe it was hand knit, such was its quality and neatness.

Pat Garner, another of the army of Weardowney knitters, embodies the vast experience and history these foot soldiers of knitting have. Her

recollections of knitting are typical of those of the knitters working for Weardowney, many of whom have individually fascinating stories of how they started knitting and how Weardowney has provided a new forum for their skills.

"My first recollection of knitting was at infant school. We were given a ball of wool, some steel knitting needles, and a piece of wire wool. We had to clean the rust off the needles before we could learn to knit!

"At this time the family used to sit around my grandmother's kitchen table knitting dishcloths out of cotton (more like soft string) and seaboot stockings for the Merchant Navy on the Atlantic run. These stockings were in thick, oiled wool and

were dreadful to knit. However, as they were supposed to keep the seamen dry and warm (I don't know if they did!), we felt we were doing our bit for the war effort.

"During my teens and twenties I began knitting fashionable garments, usually from *Vogue Knitting* magazine, which was absolutely wonderful.

"In the fifties and sixties there was always more than one wool shop in each town. As knitters didn't always have the money to buy a complete batch of yarn, these shops had a 'lay-by' at the back of the counter. The 'lay-by' was a system whereby you chose your yarn, purchased enough to get started and were given a ticket, then the yarn was kept for one month. This enabled you to buy your yarn a bit

"Weardowney...

at a time and be sure that you had the right dye lot. Unfortunately, most of these small wool shops have disappeared, along with many of the magazines that offered wonderful patterns.

"Thank heavens for Weardowney, at last I am able to knit designer garments in beautiful yarns, not the acrylics that have become the norm."

Weardowney is both part of, and a driving force in, the resurgence of hand knitting as a pastime and as a fashion textile. Their efforts to conserve and continue the tradition are unwavering. They are leading a renewed interest in the craft, one that many communities have been struggling to save. Only recently the National Trust of Scotland had two houses to rent on the island of Fair Isle,

available at only £300 (about US$600) a year. In advertising them the Trust highlighted the island community's hope of trying to make up the shortfall of skilled knitters—the demand for Fair Isle knits far outweighing the community's ability to produce them—and wanted to rent the houses to knitters.

Weardowney both encourages and maintains the tradition of hand knitting, but is also fashion forward, producing contemporary design that is far removed from the 1970s "knit-your-own-yogurt" approach to the craft. Weardowney has helped make hand knitting relevant again.

The Birth and Evolution of Knitting

The history of the birth of knitting, and the subsequent evolution of the discipline, has still to be definitively researched and written. However, pop anthropology would tell us that soon after man could hunt, kill, and wear skins as clothing, the necessity of creating clothes would perhaps lead to picking up a piece of fiber and playing with it, twisting and turning, eventually leading to the production of basic fabric. The first man-made materials had to be produced by hand, by the manipulation of singular elements into material— why not by knit?

Examples of early yarn—some of the best preserved being Egyptian dating between 2000 and 1700 BC—were manipulated with wooden spindles and woven. Surviving needles are for sewing and netting, but knitting needles don't appear until much later. Mary Thomas, Britain's best-loved authority on knitting, almost despairs in her research, as early knitting relics are more rare than those for any other type of textile.[1] Some literary evidence exists, but in the form of legend. In Homer's *Odyssey*, Penelope, waiting for her husband Odysseus (presumed dead) to return, fends off other suitors by claiming she cannot remarry until she has finished a shroud for her father-in-law, Laertes. Working on it every day, she undid it at night, buying time for her love to come back to her. Although the usual translation has the shroud being woven, it has been suggested that her trick would only be possible with a knitted garment, as undoing a woven garment would damage the thread and reveal her secret. This theory is doubted by Richard Rutt, the foremost authority on hand knitting, as there is no Greek word for "knit," making it as historically invalid as the Yemeni legend that Eve, in the Garden of Eden, knitted the pattern on the serpent's back.[2]

---

1. Thomas, Mary; *Mary Thomas's Knitting Book*, Dover Pulications, 1972, p.1 **2**. Rutt, Richard; *A History of Hand Knitting*, Interweave Press, Inc., 1987, p.27

So who invented knitting? Most literary evidence points to weaving being the first fabric. Pliny the Elder in *Historia Naturalis* considered the "Egyptians to be the inventors of the art of weaving," and all biblical references are also for woven fabrics.[3] So, for concrete examples of the origins of knitting, we must look to archaeological evidence, and though the Egyptians are popularly thought to be the inventors, the earliest fragment is Syrian.

Yale University has the earliest known fragment of knitted wool fabric in existence. It comes from the ancient Syrian city of Dura Europos, and dates from around 250 AD. Yale has three fragments, and though we still do not know what type of garment they could be from, they are most definitely wool, and knitted. They are ribbed and made using nalbinding—the technique of knitting using one needle, and a forerunner of modern knitting. Made of undyed yarn, with colored bands running through the middle of each, the fragments are worked in what has been described as the "crossed Eastern Stitch," and display part of an elaborate pattern.[4]

Dura Europos was destroyed by the Persians in 256 AD, and the conquerors, being focused on loot and gold, ignored clothing as unimportant and it was luckily buried with the city under the dry, preserving, and protecting desert sands—the reason for the fragments' survival.[5]

Although from this evidence there would be reason to believe that the Syrians were the inventors of knitting, it has been suggested that as Dura was a fortress city, it was also a "caravan city"—a place where caravans passing to and from the east and west stopped, with traders bringing goods to the active marketplaces and bazaars.[6] It is therefore possible that knitting was practiced elsewhere and the knit fragments were, in fact, imports. The acknowledgement of the fragments as nalbinding is relatively recent, bringing up an important point in establishing examples of early knit—often archaeologists cannot distinguish between types of fabric. They can categorize material as textiles in general, but without expert analysis earlier examples of knitting may have slipped through the cracks and could actually exist.

The next landmark in the birth of knitting is Coptic knitting, as developed by the Egyptians. The Victoria & Albert Museum holds five examples of Coptic knitting—four socks and a doll's cap. Coptic knitting is also a single-needle type of knitting and is practically the same as nalbinding. It is thought to be an extension of basketry or netting technique and is slow to accomplish due to the short lengths of yarn it employs.[7] Analyzing Coptic knitting gives credence to the possibility of the birth of knitting being much earlier than the physical evidence suggests. Single-needle knitting most likely existed before spinning truly emerged. This tallies up with the pop anthropology discussed earlier: if only short lengths of matter were available—such as reeds, stems of grasses, strips of animal fur—then the technique of spinning probably developed from rolling new and old lengths together and then applying the single-needle technique.[8]

The Egyptian sock illustrated opposite is from the fourth or fifth century AD and shows considerable technical skill. Made from dyed red yarn in a crossed stocking stitch, the sock displays the development from single-needle to the more familiar two-needle knitting. It is knitted from the top of the sock down to the heel, in the round to the instep, and the toe section is knitted separately and looped onto the main part of the foot.[9] With its adaptability of shape, and ability to mimic the human form in a flexible way, it is easy to see how knitting was to become such an important part of textile development.

Most of the examples of Coptic and Egyptian knitting are socks, basic in shape with a split toe for sandals. Thus early knitting was for essential

3. Grass, Milton. N; *The Origins of the Art of Knitting*, Archaeology, VIII, Autumn 1955, p.185   **4.** Ibid.   **5.** Ibid.   **6.** Ibid.   **7.** Burnham, Dorothy; *Coptic Knitting, an Ancient Technique*, Textile History, vol.3, Dec, 1972   **8.** Ibid.   **9.** Levey, S.M; *Illustrations of the History of Knitting Selected from the Collection of the Victoria & Albert Museum*, Textile History, vol.1, no. 2, 1969, p.184

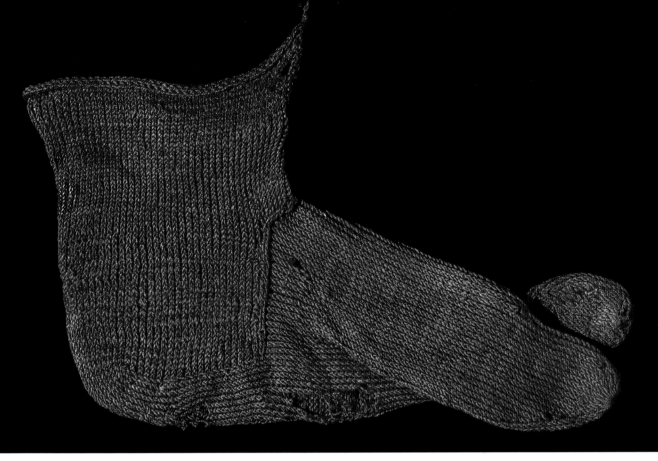

This early Egyptian knitted sock has a divided toe section to accommodate the wearer's sandals. To the contemporary eye it looks rather like a Japanese tabi sock, which also has a divided toe for sandals.

garments—for the working elements of the ancient wardrobe—and was used across the classes. It was when the practice of knitting moved to Europe that we see it become more elaborate and decorative, changing its purpose and use in fashion, and changing in social currency.

Knitting moved from Arabia to Egypt and back again with the invasion and conquer of Egypt by the Arabs in 641 AD.[10] The introduction of knitting to Europe has two hypotheses: one is the introduction of Coptic knitting through Islamic art and culture permeating Southern Spain, brought with the conquering Arabs to the Iberian Peninsula in the seventh century. The second hypothesis has it arriving with Christian Coptic missionaries on journeys and pilgrimages from Egypt to Spain and Italy.[11] Whichever is the correct theory, by the early eleventh and twelfth centuries knitting as an art and practice was well established in various countries across Europe.

Once imported to Europe, the development of knitting really took off. Assimilated into European culture, knitting became not only a craft, but an art, a skill that could be mastered and progressed, developing into that which we recognize today and gaining in importance as a respected ability. The history of knitting prior to, and during, the Renaissance is inextricably linked to the display of wealth. Surviving examples of knit from the eleventh through to the sixteenth centuries were made for the wealthy, either royalty and aristocracy, or that other bastion of European wealth, the Church.

Single-needle knit survived the development of two-needle knitting as a complex and discernable

10. Grass, Milton. N; *The Origins of the Art of Knitting*, Archaeology, VIII, Autumn 1955, p.188   **11.** Ibid.

Above Magnificent silk gloves made
to be worn by royalty.

Opposite *Buxtehude Madonna* by Master Bertram of
Minden c.1390.

display of virtuosity. Knitting had fully developed from nalbinding to two-needle knitting somewhere between the fifth and tenth centuries, the present thin scholarship leaving us with this five-hundred-year window. However, the decorative fabric that mastery of single-needle knitting could achieve assured its survival.

This quality of work, and its difficulty, inferred a sense of opulence. Silk gloves found on the body of Henry III in Speyer Cathedral, Germany, are a prime example of this. Henry was the son of Emperor Conrad II, who built the Romanesque cathedral from 1030–62 as an Imperial resting place, with Henry being only the second in a long line of Germanic monarchs to be interred there. Such a fabulous display of enormous wealth and power was meant as testament to their dynasty and thus only the finest funereal apparel would do. The silk gloves are the result of months of painstaking work, with 6–8 rows and 12–16 stitches per centimeter; they display the wealth and status of the wearer as effectively as any magnificent jewelry.[12]

Indeed, much of the history of hand knitwear before the eighteenth century concerns display of wealth and status. That is not to say that knitting was not being practiced in a more domestic and modest arena, but the scarce pieces that survive are precious items that were valuable and thus given due care—everyday garments in most areas of textile history do not survive due to lack of value and, more simply, their destruction through wear. There is also no documentary evidence, as scenes of domestic life and the depiction of anyone but the aristocracy or religious figures did not truly appear in art history until the realism of Dutch genre painting in the seventeenth century.

There are a few fourteenth-century paintings that depict the practice of knitting, known as the "knitting Madonnas." These show the Virgin and child in a more domestic and more human light. They were representations of, and venerations to, the virgin's humility and natural motherhood. However, as Richard Rutt so rightly points out, we cannot take this as being representative of how knitting fitted into fourteenth-century life.[13] The pictures do not tell us whether both the rich and the poor practiced knitting, or give any indication as to whether it was a leisurely pursuit. We can assume that it must have been associated with femininity and female virtue, but perhaps also a sense of diligence and industry.

The Holy Family (c.1345, Abegg Collection, Berne), attributed to the Sienese painter Ambrogio Lorenzetti (1290–1348), is one of the first "knitting Madonnas." Mary knits in the round with four

12. Burnham, Dorothy; *Coptic Knitting, an Ancient Technique*, Textile History, vol.3, Dec, 1972, p.122 13. Rutt, Richard; *A History of Hand Knitting*, Interweave Press, Inc., 1987, p.44

needles, with what appears to be a "lazy susan" at her feet, the Christ child at her knee, and Joseph looking on. Though it may not tell us a lot about the practice of knitting and its place or development in Northern Italy, we can read it as saying that knitting was at least an activity that was honorable enough for the Mother of God to be seen practicing, and thus a worthy craft.

The best known of the "knitting Madonnas" is the *Buxtehude Madonna* (c.1390, Kunsthalle, Hamburg), also known as the *Visit of the Angels*, by Master Bertram of Minden (1367–1415). It shows the Virgin with the Christ child again at her feet, though here He lies on the grass reading a book, with Mary finishing a sleeved garment that she has knitted in the round on four needles. This is the seamless robe taken from Christ before his crucifixion (the garment is unclear in the Lorenzetti painting), the artist assuming it had to be knitted for it to be seamless (refuted by Rutt).[14] Her devotion and the appeal of motherhood is represented through her industry in knitting for her child, with the lingering purpose of the garment that she is making poignantly hanging in the air. The grand throne and windowed canopy behind her tell the viewer of her status as Queen of Heaven. Knitting thus plays its role by placing the Virgin in the realm of the real.

The Church was to be a driving force for knitting for the next couple of hundred years. Some of the best existing examples of hand knitting encompass relic purses, priest's girdles and ecclesiastical gloves. The Victoria & Albert Museum have two wonderful examples of sixteenth-century Spanish gloves, though they are not a pair. Both are made from red silk and silver-gilt thread in stockinette stitch and are finished with silver and silver-gilt lace and plaited braid.[15] With their luxurious declarations of faith in the form of an embroidered silver cross and the christogram "IHS," they assert the power of the Church in highly material manner.

Above A sixteenth-century felted cap from the collection of the Victoria & Albert Museum.
Opposite There are no pictures of Queen Elizabeth's legs, but we know she wore both wool and silk stockings.

Despite the importance of religious knitted items, knitted garments had gradually become part of everyday life and the fifteenth century saw knitwear become a staple of the everyday wardrobe. The most popular item was the felt cap. These could be round and flat, circular with some height, or any number of shapes. The felting process of the fifteenth century entailed the un-dyed knit be finished, then it would be dyed, soaked for four days, and when the wool thickened, it would be blocked, brushed, or cut into shape.[16]

In Britain the manufacture of caps was controlled by Parliament, suggesting an industry of such size and importance that it had to be regulated. An act of Henry VII in 1488 set the price of felted hats at 1s 8d, and knitted woollen caps at 2s 8d—wool being a shilling more expensive. The cappers act of 1571 declared that every person above the age of six in the cities, towns, villages, or hamlets of England shall wear on Sundays and holidays "a cap of wool, thick and dressed in England, made within this realm, and only dressed and finished by some of the trade of cappers, upon pain to forfeit for every day of not wearing 3s. 4d."[17] As if to compound the demarcation of more

---

14. Rutt, Richard; *A History of Hand Knitting*, Interweave Press, Inc., 1987, p.48 **15.** Levey; *Textile History*, 1969, p.185 **16.** Thomas, Mary; *Mary Thomas's Knitting Book*, Dover Publications, 1972, p.4
17. Levey; *Textile History*, 1969, p.189

Above and opposite: Hand knitting was always part of the home lives of the working classes, as these wonderful early photographs of Cornish girls, above, and French women, opposite, show.

the individual would submit masterpieces to the guild for his acceptance into it; there were thirteen weeks in which to prepare these pieces. Mary Thomas explains the masterpieces required[18]: The first was a carpet "4 ells square" (around 1.9m by 1.6m), with a design to contain flowers, foliage, birds, and animals in natural colors. The second was to knit a beret, the third a woollen shirt, and the fourth a pair of hose with Spanish clocks. The carpet was the most scrutinized of all the pieces, being the most complicated and costly.

Becoming a master, and member of any guild, was of great significance and benefit to the individual. In the days long before a welfare state, the guilds would look after the member and his family in terms of healthcare, education, and supporting them in trade. Trade restrictions were in place all across Europe and were controlled by the guilds—knitting guilds acted in exactly the same way as those for silversmiths or goldsmiths.

Knitted masterpieces emerged from Bohemia in the 1560s, Bohemia eventually being battered into releasing the secrets of the work by administrative law passed by Austria and Germany. Southern Germany, along with Silesia and Alsace, were particularly forceful in their requirements and statutes. Along with heavy joining fees, the high standards required for the masterpieces were purposefully excessive, since by imposing such standards the guilds were able to regulate their growth, the supply of goods on the market, and thus the market itself.[19] These extraordinarily high levels of quality mean that we can be grateful for some of the wonderful pieces that survive. The example in the City Hall at Breslau, Wroclaw, from 1674 is spectacular, with a central cartouche of the risen Christ bordered by twenty-one coats of arms of the city council in vivid colors.[20]

Guilds continued to exert their power throughout the sixteenth and seventeenth centuries. In England, the main focus of knitting

ordinary knitwear being for the lower half of the feudal pile, exempt from this law were the nobility and anyone of good birth and title. The forcing of people to buy their caps from a proper "capper," registered to the trade, signifies perhaps the most important development in hand knitting—the rise of the guild.

Knitting guilds seem to have been operating from around the fourteenth century. They were essential to the development of knitting, with the push for expertise leading to improvement in technique and advancement of the craft.

The guild system was orientated towards the Court and the Church, focusing on finery such as gloves and hose, and was also entirely male. Apprenticeships lasted seven years, after which

18. Thomas, Mary; *Mary Thomas's Knitting Book*, Dover Publications, 1972, p.2 **19.** Turnau I. and Ponting K.G.; *Knitted Masterpieces*, Textile History, vol.7, 1976, p.8 **20.** Illustrated in Rutt; p.91

activity was stockings and hosiery, garments that define the beginning of knitwear. As silk hose from Spain became more readily available, stockings became more outlandish and luxurious and the English market improved. Hose were the foundation for costume well into the eighteenth century. Queen Elizabeth I was only introduced to silk stockings around 1576 and switched from wool because silk was deemed far softer (undoubtedly, given wool processes at the time). [21] Fashion truly dictated knit for the first time, as the court style for extremely short trunks required a sheer knit—easily made from silk but, as techniques improved, also possible with fine worsted. William Shakespeare, in his *Two Gentlemen of Verona*, mentions "knit" twice, with the two comic servants, Launce and Speed, jesting about Launce's lover knitting him a stocking— "knit" had entered the lexicon of English.[22]

The guilds were to suffer a fatal blow with the invention of the stocking frame by William Lee in 1589. The frame was the first step towards the Industrial Revolution and would affect hand knitters the most. This was despite the efforts of Queen Elizabeth herself, who refused to grant a patent to Lee on the grounds that she had "too much love for my poor people who obtain their bread by the employment of knitting."[23] However, it was the beginning of the end for the monopoly that hand knitters had on the industry, certainly in England. As often happens with such a revolutionary invention, whether permitted or not, the technology was out and the introduction of stock-frame knitting, in combination with foreign imports, drove hand knitting into the home. The "Worshipful Company of Framework Knitters" was founded in July 1657, and William Lee died penniless in France, having not profited from his endeavor.[24]

21. Rutt, Richard; *A History of Hand Knitting*, Interweave Press, Inc., 1987, p.68 **22**. Ibid, p.6 **23**. Levey; *Textile History*, 1969, p.190 **24**. Hartley M. and Ingilby J.; *The Old Hand-knitters of the Dales*, Dalesman Publishing Co. Ltd., rev. edn 2001, p.9, p.7

Les Tricoteuses Jacobines, ou de Robespierre. Elles étoient un grand nombre à qui l'on donnoit 40 Sols par jour pour aller dans la tribune des Jacobins applaudir les motions sléérokitionnaires. An 2.

JACOBIN vociférant une Motion à la Tribune.

LE BONET ROUGE. Beaucoup de Citoyens craignans d'être denoncés comme moderés s'affubléront du Bonet Rouge! Les femmes rioient de voir leur mari si élegamant coëffés.

Above: The Tricoteuses, women who sat beside the guillotine and knitted an awful accompaniment to executions, were a reality that became the stuff of dark legend.

Opposite: Though nowadays a mainly female pursuit, knitting was for generations an honorable male preserve.

Lee's breakthrough resulted in a thriving cottage industry in Nottinghamshire and Leicestershire, which gradually ate away at the hand-knit industry. Hand knitting still continued throughout the seventeenth century and garments were hand knitted alongside hose. A particularly beautiful example is the sky-blue silk "waistcoat" worn by King Charles I to his execution on the January 30, 1649. The waistcoat (by modern definition more a knitted shirt), is now at the Museum of London and is extraordinary for its extremely fine hand-knit gauge in a damask pattern. The garment's history is made even more special by Charles' famous request to be sure of its being warm—in order to stop him shaking with the cold and the people mistaking this for fear.

By the turn of the eighteenth century, hand knitters were really feeling the pinch. The novelist Daniel Defoe (1660–1731) wrote *Giving Alms No Charity* in 1704, about the sad decline of Norwich and its hand knitters: "Men on the knitting frame perform that in a day which could otherwise employ a poor woman eight or ten days."[25] In the later *A Tour Through the Whole Island of Great Britain* (1724–6), he became further irritated for the poor, and the decline of hand knitting: "[Stourbridge, now Stourminster] was once famous for making the best stockings in England; but that trade now is much decayed by the increase of the knitting-stocking engine or frame."[26]

In the eighteenth century, as hand knitting lost its reign and slipped ever down the social scale,

---

25. Rutt, Richard; *A History of Hand Knitting*, Interweave Press, Inc., 1987, p.86   **26.** Ibid, p.87

Coco Chanel—the first
true knitwear designer.

Knit into Fashion

Up until the beginning of the twentieth century the concept of fashion existed, but not in the way we know it today. The development of the contemporary notion of fashion is a large topic not within the scope of this book, but in terms of the incorporation of knit into fashion, knitwear being regarded as "fashion" is tied inextricably to the birth of fashion after the First World War.

The emergence of fashion houses in the late nineteenth century began with Charles Frederick Worth (1825–1895), a dressmaker who was the first to sew labels into his clothes and who created the first *maison couture* (fashion house). He thus raised himself to being a designer, rather than just a dressmaker. He was the first to be described as a *couturier* and this marked the point in time from which customers would be led by the designs of others, rather than approaching their tailor or seamstress with what they wanted.

However, Worth did not introduce knitwear into fashion, only the idea of the "designer." Knitted items were still at the bottom of the fashion pecking order in Victorian dress. For the upper and middle classes, knit was either for utility items (hose, undergarments) or accessories (scarves, gloves, bags), but for the working man and woman, knitwear was a key wardrobe staple, being both practical and affordable. It was not until after the First World War, and the development of a more relaxed way of wearing clothes, that knitwear increased in status.

Gabrielle "Coco" Chanel was the first *couturière* to incorporate knitwear fully into her collections. Her work came at a point in fashion history when clothes became more liberated—because of physical demands of the wearer as well as individual aesthetics—and indeed, she is considered a large influence in this revolution. Elsa

Schiaparelli swiftly followed Chanel in the late 1920s and was a key figure in pushing knitwear even further: Schiaparelli's hand knits were the celebrity handbag of their day—everyone had to have one. Chanel and Schiaparelli, each in their own manner, were hugely influential in helping knitwear into the modern wardrobe, translating it from men's sportswear into women's wear, both formal and informal.

Coco Chanel (1883–1971)

Gabrielle "Coco" Chanel was born into a poor family in the Loire in 1883. Having spent most of her childhood in an orphanage, she then spent much of her adult life escaping her impoverished background. Her reticence in discussing her childhood means that we know very little about her training in fashion. She was certainly taught to sew at the convent and most likely was also taught to knit there—both being essential skills for a young girl at that time. These skills were to be her passport out of poverty. While working as a tailor's assistant she met Etienne Balsan, a textile heir who brought her to his estate near Compiègne.[1] It was here, amongst Balsan's wealthy friends, that she delighted in being a modern sportswoman.

She dressed up in masculine styles, taking her lead from the French respect for British tailoring at the time and the modern wish to live an active life. The men's clothes she wore were often sporting clothes left around by Balsan's friends—she was a "fashionista" of sorts, utilizing what was available and incorporating things into her own style.

Moving to Paris to become a milliner, she began Chanel Modes at 21 Rue Cambon in about 1910.[2] By the beginning of the First World War Chanel had made a name for herself with her pared-down millinery, such a contrast to the enormously frothy hat decorations we so equate with Edwardian excesses. The war made her—she took a shop in Deauville, the seaside resort on Normandy's Côte

Fleurie, and it was in this wealthy leisure town that she discovered her market for comfortable sportswear for men and women. Her first success, and first signature item, was the "Chanel sweater," sold in Deauville around 1913.

Much of Chanel's history in this period is hearsay and conjecture, such as the anecdote in which Chanel, feeling cold, picked up a polo player's sweater, belted it, and pushed up the sleeves to make it fit properly.[3] Having decided that this would look chic if tailored for a female physique, she made some up for her shop and the Tricot Marinière were an instant sell-out. This story would certainly tally with her enjoyment of a more masculine, comfortable, personal style. By 1917 the loose-fitting sweater, often with a "sailor collar" and matching belt, was fashionable around the world. The "Chanel sweater" appeared in American *Vogue* in 1917 and is noted as a "slip-over sweater."[4]

Importantly, the *Vogue* illustration (rather than a photograph) was interpreted in emerald-green silk jersey. Chanel was instrumental in the introduction of jersey fabric into the language of fashion. It was a textile primarily used, as with most knit, for undergarments, but Chanel saw its potential as a versatile fabric for outer garments. Indeed, with her early work liberating the modern woman from the fashion of constraint in order to pursue outdoor activity, she heralded the approaching death knell of the corset, the proportions of which had become almost comical in the pursuit of the ever-disappearing Edwardian waist.

In short, by embracing knitted fabrics for sportswear, Chanel had stumbled upon one of the key reasons for knit's existence as a textile—its flexibility. Knit has an ability to mimic and form shape without extensive cutting and intricate panelling. The early Chanel designs, with their emphasis on flexibility for sports such as bathing or playing tennis, were a driving force in creating an entirely new way of wearing clothes for women, as

1. Madsen, Axel; *Chanel: A Woman of her Own*, Owl Books, 1991 **2.** de la Haye and Tobin; *Chanel: the Couturière at Work*, V&A Publications, 1994, p.10 **3.** Ibid, p.16 **4.** Ibid. p.13

well as offering an appealing and chic silhouette: "I make fashions women can breathe in, feel comfortable in, and look younger in," she once said.[5] Ingrid Sischy goes as far as claiming this as an early feminist victory and though Chanel was not politically motivated, she did, to a certain extent, liberate women from constrictive costume.[6] One could argue that this turn towards a masculine aesthetic was one step on the road towards equality. Chanel, and her "Garçonne" look, had a wider influence that she could ever have imagined.

Applying jersey to sportswear was a first step in her many innovations. In a sense her experiments with knitwear and knitted fabrics spawned the Chanel style. Following her expansion of the use of jersey into dresses, practical for their lightweight properties, Chanel moved into other areas. Her sleek silhouettes encouraged a whole generation of women into streamlined clothes. The 1920s saw the birth of the classic Chanel suit and Karl Lagerfeld, head of the House of Chanel today, is still making the suit in similar proportions to the twenties original—using wool to create a slim skirt and round-necked jacket that is the quintessence of Chanel's chic minimalism.

Chanel's help in the introduction of the sweater into women's fashion is proven in a song of 1920 that points to the height of the "jumper craze." (A sweater is referred to as a jumper in the UK.) "All the Girls are Busy Knitting Jumpers" by R.P. Weston and Burt Lee was enormously popular and came out of the post-war change from knitting for the troops to knitting for personal use.[7] More illustrative was a British hit by Hermann Lohr and F.R. Burrow, performed in 1919:

Wherever you are, wherever you go,
In Piccadilly or Pimlico,
Nothing but jumpers will you see,

A classic Schiaparelli coat with a geometric design in bold, contemporary colors.

Encircling Femininity.

Jumpers color'd in every hue,
Jumpers scarlet and green and blue,
Jumpers purple and pink and puce,
Jumpers clingy and jumpers loose,

5. Ewing, Elizabeth; *History of 20th Century Fashion*, Batsford, 2001, p.100   6. Sischy, Ingrid; *100 Most Influential People of the Twentieth Century*, Time, June 8, 1998   7. Rutt, Richard; *A History of Hand Knitting*, Interweave Press, Inc., 1987, p.140

Elsa Schiaparelli combined an innovative eye for colour and design with practicality in her inspiring garments.

Jumpers stripey and jumpers plain,
Jumpers that drive you quite insane.
Some with collars and some without,
Some for the thin and some for the stout,
Some with bobbles and some with belts,
Some with fringes (are these for the Celts?),
Some fluffed up like the fur of a rabbit—
Oh! Ev'ry one's got the jumper habit![8]

Britain and France had suffered great manufacturing losses during the war and the textile industries had been heavily hit. People turned to practical ways of creating fabrics, the most popular and accessible being hand knitting. With an abundance of patterns from publications such as *Woolcraft* alongside the cult of physical activity and the fashion for sportswear as casual wear, knitting enjoyed a renaissance.

In 1924 Chanel designed costumes for Diaghilev's ballet *Le Train Bleu*. Dancers were seen in hand-knitted bathing costumes and imitation Fair Isle jersey.[9] Both male and female dancers wore the costumes and the unisex designs were to prove daring, but received a hugely warm reception in both Paris and London. The ballet was built around the athletic games at Deauville and the classic Chanel palette of black and white was used to charming effect. The golfing costume aped the Fair Isle jumpers for men that were popularized by the Prince of Wales. Though these costumes were all hand knitted, generally available sportsclothes, such as bathing costumes, became increasingly sleek and were mostly machine knitted. Chanel's ballet designs are an early example of knitwear meeting high art. Elsa Schiaparelli, the other key practitioner of knit in the 1920s and 1930s, took this even further—her designs are close to works of art themselves.

Elsa Schiaparelli (1890–1973)

Elsa Schiaparelli is often, and somewhat unfairly, described as the second leading *couturière* of the 1920s and 1930s after Chanel. Certainly her house did not survive like the fashion behemoth that is the House of Chanel today (though had it not been for a mid-1950s revival, the same fate might have overtaken Chanel), nor did she have the same global press coverage that Chanel received, but we forget just how successful Schiaparelli was. In 1930 the turnover of her establishment on the Rue Cambon was an estimated one hundred and twenty million francs a year and she employed two thousand people in her twenty-six workrooms.[10]

Schiaparelli came late to the world of fashion; her first encounter with it was not until 1924 when, aged thirty-four and on a trip to escape her failing marriage, she met the *couturier* Paul Poiret in Paris.[11] With his encouragement she began to design her own clothes, then to freelance,

8. Blackman, Cally; *Handknitting in Britain from 1908–39: the work of Marjory Tillotson*, Textile History, 177–200, 1998, p.188.   9. Rutt, Richard; *A History of Hand Knitting*, Interweave Press, Inc., 1987, p.141   10. Laver, James; *Costume and Fashion*, Thames and Hudson, 1996, p.235
11. Blum, Dilys E.; *Shocking! The Art and Fashion of Elsa Schiaparelli*, Yale University Press, New Haven, 2003, p.11

eventually launching her own collection in 1927. Her salon, "Stupidir le Sport," was an immediate hit, and her signature pieces were all knitted. Schiaparelli, unlike Chanel, began with knit, so much so that by August of 1928 *The New Yorker* magazine declared, "Schiaparelli, after all, belongs to knitted sweaters, or they to her."[12]

Schiaparelli's first collection concentrated on hand-knitted wool jackets in grey and sweaters in strong geometric designs. They were in block colors, bold and imaginative, some with accents in metal thread. These sweaters made Schiaparelli popular; they represented modern, clean design— no doubt a break from the dazzling home-knitted designs that the "jumper craze" so epitomized.

The most famous of the sweaters is the *trompe l'oeil* sweater of the 1927 November collection. By this stage she had nearly a year of designing and refining her patterns under her belt and her experiments with visual tricks, inspired by her friendships with leading artists combined with an enthusiastic rebelliousness, were significant factors in the avant-garde influences she incorporated into her work. The *trompe l'oeil* sweater appears to have a white bow hanging down, a scarf drawn around the neck, and white cuffs, contrasting with the black main body. In fact, it is all one garment, hand knitted by Armenian women in Paris.[13]

The design isn't the only key to the sweater's success. The unusual stitch that the Armenian women used, "a steady stitch" as Schiaparelli described it, was able to hold its shape better than other hand knits of the period.[14] It was this sweater that led to the first orders from American department stores, securing her popularity and gaining her a more global consumer base.

Schiaparelli's inventiveness with the sweater continued into 1928 and her collection in January of that year saw a strengthening of her use of *trompe l'oeil* as a signature motif. Her designs included knitted inserts that suggested belts, and knitted-in scarves slung around the hip, which stood out from the main garment and gave a further sense of texture. There were also one- and two-piece bathing suits, "beach pajamas" (to wear over bathing suits), hand-knitted coats and skirts, crocheted berets, and a *trompe l'oeil* sweater with knitted-in collar and tie (a look that was revived commercially on T-shirts in the 1980s).[15] Thus were accessories incorporated into the design, completing the whole look and leaving the wearer with less to worry about in terms of dressing the garment up. Ready-to-wear (though the concept was in its infancy) was being crossed with *haute couture* in a pioneering way. "Schiaparelli pour le sport" was hung above the shop, marking her designs as modern apparel for the modern woman.

What directly influenced the *trompe l'oeil* motif has yet to be fully researched. Certainly, before her arrival in Paris she knew influential artists, coming into contact with the Dadaists in New York, and Gabrielle Picabia (the wife of Francis Picabia) remained a lifelong friend. In his autobiography *Self Portrait*, the surrealist painter and photographer Man Ray writes of an incident with Schiaparelli's husband at the avant-garde chess club the Pepper Pot, in which he came to blows with a chess master. Later, in the 1930s, Schiaparelli collaborated with many surrealists, notably Salvador Dali, for her "lobster dress," worn by several leading fashionable women (including, famously, the Duchess of Windsor).

Schiaparelli started with, and owed her fame to, hand knitwear, but she did slowly move away from knit into experimenting with new fabrics and techniques, especially new man-made fabrics such as rayon. However, her beginnings in knit never entirely left her from a design point of view, and her early work undoubtedly sowed the seed for her inventiveness and innovations in shape, silhouette, and texture. The summer collection of 1932

---

12. Blum, Dilys E.; *Shocking! The Art and Fashion of Elsa Schiaparelli*, Yale University Press, New Haven, 2003, p.13   **13.** Ewing, Elizabeth; *History of 20th Century Fashion*, Batsford, 2001, p.116   **14.** Blum, Dilys E.; *Shocking! The Art and Fashion of Elsa Schiaparelli*, Yale University Press, New Haven, 2003, p.13   **15.** Ibid, p.14.

included a dark red crepe evening dress with an asymmetrical, crinkly, silk-ribbon scarf in coral, draped and bowed just under the shoulder, harking back to the knitted *trompe l'oeil* scarves on the sweaters in her first collection.[16]

Not only did she pioneer in the aesthetics of knit, Schiaparelli also did not overlook practicality. One such example is a patented bathing suit that incorporated a brassiere, invisible to the eye, with straps crossing low at the back and wrapped discreetly around the front.[17] Her talent for clever infrastructure, here a form of early sports bra, added to the genius of her original designs.

Though her use of hand knitwear could be seen as limited to her sweaters and early knits, Schiaparelli's lasting legacy and influence is so much more. Her use of knit to emulate and mimic took the medium of knitting further in technique than ever before. Schiaparelli, in aesthetic and intellectual terms, pushed the boundaries of the possibilities of knit further, perhaps, than Chanel, and certainly she could be seen as the major influence on the innovations of the latter part of the twentieth century, in particular the 1970s and 1980s, especially in graphic knits.

Stylist versus designer

Twentieth-century designers known for their achievements in knitwear could be categorized into design-costumiers, genre-designers, or more simply designers and stylists of knitwear. The "designers" are innovators, pushing knitwear technically, but the "stylists," who may be trendsetters, do not necessarily push the medium to its limits in any way. Thus, a clear split in achievement is identifiable and it is the innovators who, in the history of knitwear, count the most.

A stylist par excellence is Ralph Lauren. Although a master of creating an aspirational brand and some beautiful, classic dress design, the extent of Lauren's knitwear at the beginning of his career was color coordinated socks. Fast-forwarding to his peak, when he dominated mainstream fashion with a brand that sells tradition and a romantic view of an Anglo-American lifestyle, he established himself in terms of knitting by drawing out the trend for hand knits and applying it to his own ethos, rather than the other way around. He adapted traditional stitch patterning to fit his brand and with the skill of Nancy Vale, his chief knitwear technician, Ralph Lauren became part of knitwear's history.

This is in direct contrast to the work of Schiaparelli, a true "designer" who began to design hand knitwear as that was all she could manufacture at the time, applied her innovative *trompe l'oeil,* and was thus forever considered directional. As will be clear by now, Chanel is similar to Schiaparelli historically in terms of innovation, though in subtly different fields.

Few late twentieth-century design powerhouses live up to the innovative ethos of Schiaparelli and Chanel. Like Ralph Lauren, Donna Karen could also be described as being on the "stylist" rather than "designer" side. She is primarily famous for her early "bodysuits" (1980s), and as a leading light of New York "power dressing." Her knitwear, though popular, seems to lag behind her work with fabrics. As yet, Karen has not produced knitwear that stands out as innovative or revolutionary—hence the "stylist" label.

Domestic knitting during the World Wars

It is the two World Wars that see some of the most inventive revivals of hand knit. The march of the industrial age was still affecting coastal and rural communities as their skills brought in less household revenue. The beginning of the century saw the start of the advertising of yarn. Pamphlets were produced by yarn manufacturers to popularize and add to the sales of retail yarns.

Machine-spun yarns now made publishing

---

16. Blum, Dilys E.; *Shocking! The Art and Fashion of Elsa Schiaparelli*, Yale University Press, New Haven, 2003, p.51   17. Ibid, p.27

knitwear ideas commercially viable, and the leading manufacturers began to publish these "recipe" books alongside the beginnings of women's magazines. The revolutionary element to hand knit at this time was the start of "tailoring" shapes and adapting them to fit different figures.

Patons and Baldwins, established in 1875, published *Woolcraft,* and it was an immediate success. The First World War encouraged the home-knitting trend, followed by the twenties and the rise of sportswear and jersey fabric.

Between the Wars, home knitting continued. Rationing and availability of materials forced every manufacturer, designer, and home knitter into "fashioning" garments with increased inventiveness. Unraveling worn garments, respinning them, and dyeing and working in scraps and parts of other garments created a rich seedbed of historical inspiration for designers today.

Other publications, such as Odham's *Pictorial Guide to Modern Home Knitting* and *Modern Knitting Illustrated*, taught readers how to make a fully tailored suit, an item previously only within the realm of the dressmaker or tailor. Labor-intensive techniques were championed by results, making necessary fashion garments. The reduced circumstances of the Second World War gave us one of the most creative periods in hand knit.

The Americas

The history of hand knitting in the Americas, though rich in indigenous origins, is a modern but nonetheless important one. The present-day contribution to the advancement of the craft is especially noteworthy in the United States. Works by such authors as Barbara Walker are outstanding examples of the American contribution to hand knitting. Walker's magnificent classification of stitch techniques is still in demand today, illustrating how knitting still speaks directly to the heart of American communities.

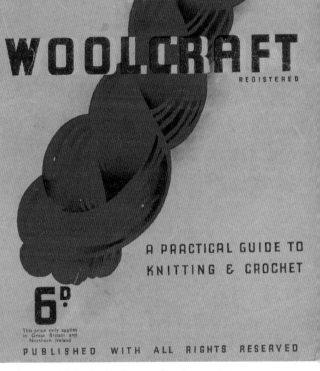

Magazines containing instructions and patterns were hugely popular with hand knitters—then and now.

The widespread understanding of a rich history, held in the knitter's hands while mastering its techniques, gives American hand knitters a humility that serves to advance the craft. Without such enthusiasts to keep it alive, the knitting tradition, as a live tradition, might not have survived. The contemporary popularity in the USA of hand crafts, needlework, and, in particular, hand knitting, with its attention to tradition and accuracy, insures that all living traditions can continue to be disseminated into the community.

John Galliano

British-born designer John Galliano (b.1960) is *haute couture's* provocateur and ringmaster. Enjoying enormous success with his own label, and at two of fashion's most important houses—a tenure as designer at Givenchy (from 1995) and presently at Christian Dior (from 1997)—Galliano is perhaps the most important designer working in *haute couture* today. His reputation has been built on an extraordinarily fertile imagination, creating dramatic new looks and statements season after season, which filter down to his ancillary collections.

To fully understand Galliano, one must never underestimate his intense passion for, and his devotion to, *haute couture*. His enormous admiration for Madame Vionnet and Charles James has influenced his vision of fashion to a great degree: they share the view that operating on this high level brings fashion into the realm of art. Galliano has a reputation for being fastidious in his approach to the quality of his products and is one of the hardest-working designers in Paris.

John Galliano's designs function on two levels: first, through his role as an image-maker, and second, through his experiments in garment construction. His early collections (in the 1980s) were styled by Amanda Grieve (now Lady Amanda Harlech, Karl Lagerfeld's muse and collaborator), and were typically theatrical, featuring elements such as stuffed birds arranged in elaborate hairstyles and presented in highly dramatized shows. This sense of the theatrical—no doubt an influence from his time as a dresser at the English National Opera—permeates his aesthetic and can often be seen in his lack of fear of pastiche or kitsch. In that respect, both Galliano and Vivienne Westwood could be seen as parodies of their own concentrated aesthetic—shown in their ever-refined visions and in their personal style.

Galliano's technical ability matches his strength of creative vision. He is a master pattern cutter and has looked to, for instance, Vionnet for cutting on the bias, and then developed such influences in new directions. Galliano has an instinctive feeling for fabric and utilizes textiles with properties that will lend themselves to his inventive shapes and forms. He also likes fabrics that are not entirely finished—that are perhaps a few stages from being fully complete. Unscoured fabrics are contrasted with textured textiles—such as smooth silk or heavy, oiled fabrics—and augment his experiments with proportion, adding textural interest.

John Galliano's relationship with hand knitwear has always been strong, and indeed, Weardowney's connection to it has not been insignificant—Gail Downey worked with him between 1983 and 1989. Gail met Galliano at the time of his first show, his infamous *Afghani Rebel* collection for his Saint Martins degree, and was commissioned to make twelve pieces of knitwear in fishermen's knit with strong cabling. Gail chose the yarn and Galliano chose the colors—Gail's stitch techniques working with Galliano's designs and shapes. After showing at the British Fashion Council's tent at London fashion week, the first orders on Galliano knitwear were upwards of £40,000. All the pieces were hand knitted, featuring Worthing and fishermen's smocks, and even the cut-and-sew garments were hand knitted, then machined.

Galliano's legacy to hand knit is the re-introduction of traditional techniques into high-fashion design. Circular knitting was, and still is, a key component of his knitted output. He leans towards the bias, thus circular knitting plays such a prominent role. His use of cable knit is a classic example of an ability to translate the traditional into fashion forward, he being one of the first designers to re-discover the technique's potential. In terms of hand knit moving other knitwear forward, Galliano's patterns would be copied by mainstream retailers, and the 2006/07 proliferation of cable-knit would not have been possible without manufacturers in the 1980s taking his lead and developing new machining techniques. Indeed, it became a challenge for the Galliano team to continually push the direction of hand knitwear, to come up with techniques and arrangements that ensured that the machine technicians had to work hard to develop the punch cards to copy the pieces for the mainstream ready-to-wear market.

Galliano's "cobweb" knit is an example of this technical and aesthetic innovation. It is an irregular lace and would have been particularly challenging for the copyists, as it has no pattern repeat. It was inspired by photocopies of lace and paper doilies and has an air of deconstruction and looseness.

The use of knit has been a constant in the work of John Galliano, his time at Dior even seeing an increase in knitwear designs. With all the great exuberance of his shows, the viewer can be dazzled by their spectacle and ignore the technical brilliance and wearability that is only seen on close inspection. Like Alexander McQueen, Galliano's successor at Givenchy, the shows that Galliano stages are set pieces, fantasy fueled by his influences, namely the theater and femininity, but they seep into all the other areas of production. Galliano continually pushes boundaries in terms of aesthetics and technique. His shows for Dior have seen the rise of the couture knitted fabric, such as that seen in his Autumn/Winter 2000/01 collection—the mohair sweater is threaded with chiffon rags and the knitted fabric can be carefully inlaid with yarns and materials.[1]

"My role is to seduce," says Galliano—and he does, skillfully combining creative force and dexterity. His ability to innovate, while retaining a sense of parody and humor, keeps his work fresh and relevant. Galliano's world of Oliver Twist, pirates, and beautifully constructed garments mark him out as a fashion revolutionary and perhaps the most important person in fashion today.

---

1. Black, Sandy; *Knitwear in Fashion*, Thames and Hudson, 2002, p.32

Jean Paul Gaultier

Jean Paul Gaultier (b.1952) is often seen as the *enfant terrible* of couture. The French designer made his name in the 1980s and early 1990s by playing with traditional concepts of fashion, inverting and deconstructing clothes with studied irreverence. After a prestigious start to his career—audaciously sending designs to Pierre Cardin and being accepted as a design assistant at the age of seventeen—he worked for Jacques Esterel and Jean Patou before launching his own label.

Gaultier is an interesting designer to look at in the context of knitwear. His reputation as a daring innovator extends beyond his well-known signature crossed-gender innovations and his place as a key exponent of power dressing. Like Galliano, Gaultier, from the beginning, imbued his designs with a sense of avant-garde theatricality. He took his cue from street fashion, adapting elements of the urban underground to create extraordinary, often challenging, shapes and constructs of garments.

Gautier's 1980s clothes came as challenging subversions to orthodox views. Taking his lead from punk in the 1970s and updating it with his own deconstructavist stamp, his presentation of gender and the way in which we view it was a challenge to all the unwritten rules that a Parisian *couturier* would usually employ. At his zenith, his representation of femininity was paraded on a global stage through his collaboration with Madonna. They appropriated an enduring image of strength in sexuality for her Blonde Ambition tour of 1990, Madonna performing in Gautier's "conical bra" designs.

The "conical bra" motif was influenced by the 1950s "sweater girl" trend towards conically stitched underwear worn under knitwear and at that time was typified as Hollywood casual wear by the actress Jane Russell. Gaultier turned the sense of brooding sexuality of that more innocent time into a confrontational sexual statement—his clothes saying as much about the wearer's individual sexuality as they did about the wearer as a sexual object of desire. Gaultier was giving sexual power to women.

It was within this revival and reinterpretation of the "sweater girl" that we see one of his most important contributions to contemporary knitwear, the revival of Aran knit. In his ready-to-wear collection of Autumn/Winter 1985/86 we see a knitted Aran dress in which he explores texture through the chunkiness of knit and applied bobbles, but which, more importantly, contains knitted conical breast-pieces[1] and sees Gaultier exploring the medium of knit to add to his vocabulary of reassessed femininity.

Much of Gaultier's work is inspired by sadomasochism, taking the feel and use of contrasting fabrics for sexual pleasure and applying them to clothes to wear, translating that enjoyment into a simple (if certainly more innocent) pleasure. The application of Aran knit to his exaggerated forms, and consequent exploration in texture, move hand knitwear forward in a quite unexpected way. Using bobbles to represent nipples on the knitted pieces is both forward-thinking and tongue-in-cheek at the same time.

The late 1990s saw Gaultier's interest in knitwear continuing to develop and his interest in texture maturing. His style at this stage had become more sedate, continuing to be highly theatrical but with less of the aggressive and sexual overtones that made him famous in the 1980s. His Autumn/Winter collection of 1998 featured beaded fishermen's sweaters and

---

1. Black, Sandy; *Knitwear in Fashion*, Thames and Hudson, 2002, p.42

elongated sweater dresses that started out in traditional cable knit at the neck and progressed down the body to the knee in changing styles, slowly unravelling to wider and more intricate knit at the hem. His use of hand-knitted bobbles and knitted chains gave the pieces a three-dimensional quality that was highly innovative.

It was not just women's wear that benefited from Gaultier's new vision of sexuality. Starting with his *L'Homme Object* collection in 1984 and developing into his first *haute couture* collection for men in 1997—traditionally an area reserved exclusively for women's wear—he presented men in a sexualized manner but not in a traditionally dominant, macho manner. Gaultier's view of men in clothing was typically narcissistic and continued to play with female sexual empowerment by making men the object of sexual desire. He did this by taking elements of the traditional male wardrobe and redesigning them to a new aesthetic. For example, he designed Fair Isle sweaters, teaming them up with skirts to create a deconstructed masculinity, twisting concepts of the traditional male role and giving them a latent passivity. This again was highly influenced by his interest in S&M.

Though not as active now as he has been, Jean Paul Gaultier continues to have an interest in new ways of looking at textiles and manipulating them aesthetically and technically. His work in the field of knitwear has been highly influential, and his hand knits are enduring and important in advancing the craft. His utilization of the medium to create pieces that fitted and said something about a body both sits well with his appreciation of form in design and demonstrates his recognition that knit is an excellent textile with which to experiment with form and shape in garments.

Kenzo

Kenzo Takada (b.1939) represents the enormous innovations that the meeting of Eastern fashion and Western fashion have achieved in the last fifty years. Having trained in Tokyo, Kenzo moved to Paris in 1964 and eventually founded his brand in 1971, emanating from his boutique Jungle Jap.

His move to Paris was well timed, as the 1960s saw a renewed interest in Eastern culture and a cultural drive towards the emergence of global influences in the arts. Kenzo married traditional Japanese shapes and colors with Western casual wear, which itself produced new shapes and colorways that were imitated throughout the 1970s and 1980s.

Kenzo made his most interesting and important contribution to fashion with knitwear. At the time Paris was experiencing the fast growth and expansion of the *prêt-a-porter* (ready-to-wear) scene. *Haute couture* dominated until the 1950s, but new habits of buying clothes and improvements in technology meant that ready-to-wear could enter the arena of "fashion" with confidence. Design-led knitwear was popular and accessible by the late 1960s, helped by the work of Sonia Rykiel in Paris. Kenzo followed in her wake to a certain extent, but his approach was fundamentally different.

Whereas Rykiel was concerned with deconstruction, Kenzo was concerned with shape and line. Along with fuller, wider skirts, he introduced deep, wide, kimono sleeves based on the traditional Japanese kimono, but he adapted the look to encourage layering. His kimono-sleeved sweaters, illustrated from 1970, demonstrate the contemporary feel of the adapted Japanese shape. Riding with the trend towards relaxed and patterned knitwear, he utilized graphic prints for the body of the pieces and applied a ribbed knit to sleeves that, with their kimono influence, flattered the arm on the diagonal. Like Rykiel, Kenzo's 1970s knitwear tended towards the tight, but he encouraged breaking up the look by wearing long-sleeved T-shirts underneath. His interest in layering continued and he began to produce shawls and further garments that were easy to mix with other pieces.

Kenzo's influence in the use of color is not to be underestimated either. From the relative restraint of his early kimono sweaters, he developed color in a way that was just as important as Missoni. Missoni concentrated on a signature pattern, but for Kenzo the purity and juxtaposition of colors were key. By mixing colors in a graphic way he achieved a sense of texture in much of his knitwear that inspired a fresh look at the way knit uses color.

Kenzo, the fashion label, is continuing to produce interesting knitwear. Though Kenzo Takada himself retired in 1993, the label got a new lease of life with the arrival of Antonio Marras in 2004. His first collection for Kenzo looked back to the essence of Kenzo's appeal—the combination of Eastern and Western culture. Included in this first collection was a kimono coat tied with a traditional Obi belt and with the house's original signature of bright colors and interest in pattern. Kenzo today is turning to a vintage style but is keeping those elements of its success in knitwear firmly in place.

Sonia Rykiel

Sonia Rykiel's (b.1930) career has been inextricably linked with knitwear. Indeed, it is the reason she went into fashion in the first place. In 1962 Rykiel was pregnant and couldn't find any soft sweatersto wear so, using one of her husband's suppliers (he owned a chic boutique in Paris called Laura), she sent off designs of her own to be made up in Venice. The resulting "poor boy sweater" was featured on the front of *Elle* magazine, sold out rapidly, and established her name in fashion. She opened her own boutique selling chic knitwear on the Left Bank in Paris in 1968, starting off with sweaters and pregnancy wear. The business expanded into a popular and enduring fashion label. Rykiel has been responsible for the development of the French style of hand knitting and was crowned "queen of knits" by American fashion bible *Women's Wear Daily* as early as the 1960s.

The "poor boy sweater" is still sold in Rykiel stores and outlets today. It got the name because, with its cropped, fitted shape and inverted seams, it could be seen as a take on a ragged sweater that one might imagine a Victorian orphan wearing, albeit more finely finished and not as distressed. It is a quintessential shape in knitwear of the late twentieth century, as its enduring appeal proves.

The 1970s saw the continuation of skinny-fit cropped sweaters, the fitted style of which, in contrast to the wide pants popular at the time, created a much sought-after slimming silhouette. The quality and shapes of the knits helped knitwear out of the fashion grave of "casualwear" and back into mainstream fashion.

Rykiel is known for her signature stripes. Although her label is now primarily run by her daughter, Nathalie, her Spring 2007 ready-to-wear collection saw Rykiel use stripes on trend shapes

for that year—the mini, the trapeze—and proclaim herself as the successor to Schiaparelli by using *trompe l'oeil* effects with knit. Three-dimensional touches were seen in the bows at the necks of dresses and swimsuits and layering around the hips, and the references to the late 1920s give an overall feel of harking back to Schiaparelli, but with a modern touch. As a testament to her sense of fun in fashion, Rykiel left the fashion journalists attending the show in an upbeat mood by instructing all the models to smile, as opposed to the somewhat serious face usually seen on the catwalk.

Rykiel also became known for her use of bold color in the 1970s and 1980s, a trait that the house still maintains today. In the Autumn/Winter collection for 2000/01 we can see color being used with bombast.[1] Shown there was a bright red angora two-piece knitted pantsuit with lace and a matching beret. The opulence in using luxurious dyed fur is another signature—Rykiel having used brightly dyed furs since the 1960s.

Alongside the styles mentioned were slogan sweaters and dresses. Rykiel was one of the first to put words onto knitted garments. She may have been unfairly described as "volatile," but "magnetic" would certainly describe her character: Andy Warhol once took 500 Polaroids of her in one day in 1986 at the Factory in New York. Rykiel's outspoken nature and daring (she has written several erotic novels involving clothes), makes her the ideal candidate for outward expression of feelings on clothes. The French people certainly celebrate her originality—she was awarded the Legion d'Honneur in 1985.

Rykiel could be said to have taken on the mantle of Schiapparelli's knitwear—from the recent developments in three-dimensional interest, adding illusion to pieces, to the sporty, slim silhouette that was so loved by the original protagonists of the 1920s "sweater craze"

movement. Although quieter in ambition and experiment than the great Schiaparelli, Rykiel nevertheless has contributed enormously to the story of hand knitting and knitwear.

---

1. Black, Sandy; *Knitwear in Fashion*, Thames and Hudson, 2002, p.50

Vivienne Westwood

Dame Vivienne Westwood (b.1941) is one of Britain's most respected contemporary designers. Credited with the invention of punk style in the 1970s, she has continued to surprise fashion critics with her often elaborate and witty creations. One of Westwood's most fascinating design traits is her tendency towards historicism. She is known for not just referencing costume history but also for displaying a knowledge of the development and construction of historic garments. The combination of the avant-garde and the traditional produces constantly innovative collections and it is her learning from the past that drives new techniques: "When you look to the past, you start to see the standards of excellence, the good taste in the way things were done, put together, formed. By trying to copy technique, you build up your own technique."[1]

In terms of knitwear, Westwood has been a key contributor to moving the medium on. Both hand knitting and machine-manufactured knitting have benefited from her visionary designs. Westwood designed knits from her very first collections. Punk in 1977 sees her experimenting with knit forms and making them her own. Traditional sweater shapes are made "punk" by the use of an extraordinarily large gauge, bright colors and over-sizing. The gauge ensures controversy if worn, as in the collection, with bare breasts underneath. The strong color palette signifies the primitivism of punk and the baggy size suggests a rebellious insolence, contradicting the delicate mohair fabric.

Early Westwood knit design would seem to start in the conceptual punk period post 1971. With Malcolm McLaren, she pushed her own style into something new and groundbreaking. Having opened the vintage record and clothes store Let it Rock, Westwood reveled in 1950s references. Describing the clothes she was making at that

---

1. Wilcox, Claire; *Vivienne Westwood*, V&A Publications, 2004, p.9

time: "I made Malcolm a pair of lurex drainpipe trousers and then I made 12 more. I started making mohair sweaters for the girls—you couldn't even buy mohair then. I loved the beatnik idea of wearing a man's sweater with tights."[2] These unraveling sweaters are the epitome of punk and deconstructed knit. Steve Jones of the Sex Pistols wore a similar one on the Anarchy in the UK tour of 1976—though it was more like a string vest than a sweater. Its subversion of the norms of knitting and the working-class associations of the string vest were typical of the punk movement.[3]

While the chunky hand knits of the *Buffalo* collection of 1983 had given way to the finer, more textured, earthy colored knits of *Nostalgia of Mud* (Autumn/Winter 1982/83), collaborations with established companies began with John Smedley for the *Witches* collection (Autumn/Winter 1983/84). In *Witches*, Westwood presented mélange underwear, the base color being black with shocking pink "witches"—Aztec-inspired graphics.[4] The harlequin leggings and twin sets of *Harris Tweed* (Autumn/Winter 1987/88), also with Smedley, are playful and subversive.

Cut and Slash (Spring/Summer 1991) sees Westwood developing her understanding and application of historical techniques. The seventeenth-century technique of slashing was a feature on fashionable hose. It is called slashing since the strips of material left open were large, looking as if someone had slashed right into them. In her *Cut and Slash* menswear, Westwood applied the slashing technique to white jeans, letting the edges fray and revealing thigh, but also knitted-in "slashes" in a zip-up cardigan. This again is typical of her subversion—the knitted fabric is not actually slashed, but is posing as such. The allusions are historical, but also hark back to her earlier punk work.

The hand knit in *Anglomania* (Autumn/Winter 1993/94) is particularly poignant. The collection, as the name suggests, refers to an obsession with all things English and in particular to the French passion for Englishness in dress during the 1780s.[5] The hand knit is in a tight, intricate lace pattern with a collar that cuts straight across the throat but has a large cut-out, exposing the cleavage. The long sleeves and tight bodice mold to the body and the garment has the specter of a corset hanging over it. The collection as a whole gives reference to Scottish woolcraft, developing the signature Westwood affair with tartan, and melds it with English historicism.

The *On Liberty* collection (Autumn/Winter 1994/95) contains Westwood's "favorite dress of all time"—a knitted dress based on Liberty & Co. archive prints of pile, needle-cord, and quilted georgette dresses. Originally designed to be worn with a "bum cushion" (a sort of bustle)[6], the dress has a brown-plum base with knitted flower details in relief and the main body of the fabric accented in gold. Westwood created the knitting pattern for the dress, which is highly complex in its delicate graduation and sculptural qualities. Also in the collection was a longer, bustle-style dress that shows hand knit's versatility beautifully. The dress is full length and slim fitting—it creates an hourglass shape without the aid of a corset—slinking down to layers of knitted flounces that run in circles from the knee down. Technically enormously accomplished, Westwood again pushed the boundaries of hand knit that bit further.

Vivienne Westwood has undoubtedly mastered hand knitwear and is still advancing it like few other contemporary designers. From her subversive punk knits to the historicist knits of her later collections, she chose to work with a medium that many avant-garde designers would not dare touch, because of the difficulty in innovation and their lack of imagination. Westwood steps up to her task with tremendous verve as one of the most exciting designers working in knit today.

---

2. Wilcox, Claire; *Vivienne Westwood*, V&A Publications, 2004, p.11   **3.** Black, Sandy; *Knitwear in Fashion*, Thames and Hudson, 2002, p.14
4. Wilcox, Claire; *Vivienne Westwood*, V&A Publications, 2004, p.69   **5.** Ibid, p.26.   **6.** Ibid, p.152

Paco Rabanne designed
costumes for cult classic
film *Barbarella*, starring
Jane Fonda

Modern Knit History

In the latter part of the twentieth century, knit finally established itself as having entered the everyday vocabulary of the wardrobe. The versatility of knit as a textile, and as a medium, was demonstrated by Chanel, Schiaparelli and the sportswear revolution of the 1920s and 1930s. The twentieth century then saw knitwear develop in new directions—designers and movements pushing it forward into new areas of its capability in fashion.

Hollywood, since its conception, has influenced the way in which we wear clothes. For knitwear, the first and most popular trend came in the 1940s and 1950s with the establishment of the "sweater girl" look. Though industrialization and the dawn of machine knit had killed off the hand knitting of hose and underwear, it was, interestingly, that industry that popularized the "sweater girl" craze. The "sweater girl" bra was the antithesis of the fashion for the flattened bust popular when Chanel and Schiaparelli brought out their iconic knits and instead reintroduced a more pronounced bust—sometimes to almost comical proportions. Its conical shape, to be revisited by Jean Paul Gaultier in the 1980s, was typically worn under tight, knitted sweaters to give women a healthy décolletage and a slimmed waist. Its popularity reached its peak in the mid 1950s, embodied by film actresses Jane Russell and Lana Turner.

Knitwear in the 1950s looked to America for its main influence. The "American casual look" was taken up by Italian clothes manufacturers and gave Italy a new and different lead over Paris.[1] Italy reintroduced the chunky knit—taking inspiration from Chanel's fishermen's jerseys and adding different styles and bold color. Large polo collars and turtlenecks, hoods, and wide armholes combined with stripes and fresh colors to provide the "Italian"

look from around 1954.[2] Looking at images of the styles, they are typical of what we imagine Middle America wore in the mid to late 1950s.

In Britain the "sloppy joe" was hugely popular and largely driven by how easy the style was to hand-knit. While the "sweater girl" style was a more challenging article to make, due to its tight, fitted shape, the "sloppy joe" had a certain amount of room for error. Hand knitting sat well with post-war frugality—for a population in reduced circumstances knitting was one way to create individual garments that were practical and could follow current fashion, without having to spend large amounts of money. However, the liberated 1960s heralded change in the direction of knitwear technology yet again, though the 1950s popular styles have developed into perennial classics still available in many variants today.

The 1960s and 1970s

The 1960s were an extraordinary time for experimentation in fashion. New designers pushed textile and garment technology to its limits to produce exciting, bright new fashion. André Courrèges (b.1923) and Paco Rabanne (b.1934) were at the forefront of this drive for invention and, though not particularly focused on knitwear, what they gave to the medium was a launch pad for further experiments with pattern and style.

Andre Courrèges opened his fashion house in 1961, but it was his 1964 "moon girl" look and 1968 space age collection that marked his place in fashion history. The "moon girl" look utilized transparent materials, plastics, and laminates to create science fiction inspired clothes. Tunics, see-through skirts, and boots were all signature items. In terms of knitwear, Courrèges experimented with

1. Ewing, Elizabeth; *History of 20th Century Fashion*, Batsford, 2001, p.170   **2.** Ibid, p.171

metallic knit, though limiting this to jackets and outerwear. However, the incorporation of ideas of transparency did lead to him making crocheted dresses that were copied throughout the 1960s.

Paco Rabanne followed a similarly space-age route and is known to a wider public for his costumes for the seminal sixties sci-fi fantasy *Barbarella* (1968). His first couture collection of 1966 challenged traditional ideas of creating garments with fabric and thread. Instead, Rabanne used metal and plastic to form a new aesthetic. His signature dresses were made from metal mesh and metal discs and links, and although they were not knitted, they did ape the knitted sweater dresses that had enjoyed popularity in the 1950s. This look, along with his and Courrèges' penchant for the transparent, created the climate from which "see-through" knit could emerge.

One of the key developments in knitwear during this period was the explosion of color and pattern. This was a result of the advances made in Italian knitwear in the late 1950s and the "colorists" emergence as a movement. The most important protagonist of this was the Italian knitwear house Missoni, founded by Ottavio "Tai" Missoni (b.1921). The late 1960s saw their signature, graphic-led colorful sweaters, dresses, and jackets come to worldwide attention. It is the boldness of Missoni's hand knits that particularly stand out. Even today the zigzag patterns that define the Missoni look are as arresting as when they were first produced and they continue to popularize the graphic-led fine-gauge knit that made their name.

Another key "colorist" who became popular in the 1960s was Kaffe Fasset (b.1937). The American-born designer settled in London in 1964 and the bright, bold color of his work was hugely influenced by his background as a painter. In 1969 *Vogue* magazine featured a David Bailey shot of his signature "tapestry pattern" knit cardigan coat and a striped sweater with a strong diagonal graphic that very much follows the vein of Missoni's treatment of knit.[3] Indeed, Missoni collaborated with Fasset early in his career, commissioning his first commercial collections. Fasset has been enormously successful, publishing on knitting and creating original patterns, though today he is predominantly known in terms of "traditional" knitting rather than contemporary fashion.

Elio Fiorucci (b.1935) started as a shoemaker but received wider recognition when he opened his store in Milan in 1967 to sell "hip" items from London and America to young Italians. His eye for bright color and internationalism mark him out as highly influential in bringing innovative fashion ideas of the time to the attention of Italian designers and thus to the Italian knitwear industry. Fiorucci was one of the first to reintroduce mohair into the lexicon of knit and his knits also pioneered the use of the "bubble"—a popular 1970s knitwear texture. In the early to mid 1970s he was key in introducing "fluoro" knits, pushing the Italian use of color in knitwear even further.

In Britain, the label and boutique Biba was influential in how fashion worked in the late 1960s and early 1970s, less in the knitwear they produced than in the way that they were trendsetters for it. Biba was one of the first to understand trends moving with young customers. Famously, the sell-out Gingham dresses, offered by mail in 1964, mark the start of the notion of a trend selling out.

In terms of knitwear, Biba popularized the use of crochet and sparked the trend for knitted cloche hats, a trend that has returned in 2007. They also led the way with the reintroduction of mohair for V-neck sweaters in the mid 1970s, combining them with pencil skirts and skinny leather ties to perpetuate the glam-rock look (following musicians such as Roxy Music and the New York Dolls), just before Vivienne Westwood took mohair and identified it with punk.

---

3. Howell, Georgina; *In Vogue, Sixty years of celebrities and fashion from British Vogue*, Penguin, 1975, p.300

A key 1960s hand-knitwear designer is Marion Foale (b.1939). Foale and Sally Tuffin collaborated after meeting at the Royal College of Art and became synonymous with good young design from 1961, as well as part of the Carnaby Street revolution with their shop Foale and Tuffin. Their beautifully tailored hand knit was a signature look, and Foale was instrumental in the move towards three-dimensional design in knitwear. She still makes hand knits today, though she moved away from Sally Tuffin in the 1970s.

The 1970s continued the trends that emerged in knitwear in the late 1960s. From the tightly fitted, short, graphic-led "poor boy sweaters" of Sonia Rykiel, to the continued influence of stylists like Biba, knit continued in fashion, cementing its place in the everyday wardrobe. The only important change in knitwear trends in the 1970s was a return to the use, and re-evaluation, of knitted jersey fabrics. In terms of their innovation, perhaps the finest protagonist was Halston (1932–1990). Halston's design aesthetic was mostly concerned with simplicity for the wearer. He appreciated natural form and became known for his unfussy, chic dresses in cashmere, silk, and rayon jersey— striving for clothes to be both comfortable and beautiful.

British designer Zandra Rhodes (b.1940) is commonly held up, quite rightly, as one of the most innovative designers working today. Her work draws heavily on color combination and, importantly, on a "calligraphic style." Her first sweater, in 1972, shows how remarkably ahead of its time her design was. Pink, green, and blue, it had bat sleeves and duck tails. The asymmetric graphics that lie across the shoulders feel almost 1980s in their design. Compared with the tight silhouettes that dominated that season, the volume on the shoulders is extraordinarily fashion forward.

The 1980s picked up where the late 1960s had started in terms of pushing techniques of hand

With stitch pattern detailing and elegant tailoring, Marion Foale's hand knits are classic pieces of design.

knitting forward. From the avant-garde, form-fitting creations of Bodymap to the exploration of the medium by John Galliano, knit in the 1980s came under much creative scrutiny. As a London store, and later a label, Joseph did much to champion new knitwear. Both Bodymap and Galliano owed their popularity to Joseph Ettedgui's (the stores' founder) keen eye for new talent. Having also progressed the career of Moschino, Joseph recognized new directional knitwear.

Bodymap was undoubtedly the most directional of Joseph's knitwear discoveries. The label only had a short lifespan—founded in 1982 and shuttered in the early 1990s—but their influence was enormous. The key to Bodymap's innovation was their passion for deconstruction in a way that was less ideological than, for example, Westwood. They turned their knits inside out, played with volume and chunky knit, and focused on new textures and forms. Graphic designs were integral to the Bodymap collections and high-contrast prints sat alongside contrasting textures.[4] Bold use of volume saw the exaggeration of shape around the body, something that they utilized in their later collaborations with contemporary dance.

The Japanese label Comme des Garçons has also been influential by way of its directional shapes, though without the multitude of textures so specific to Bodymap. The label has been going since the 1970s and came to Western fashion consciousness in the 1980s. Its founder, Rei Kawakubo, took traditional Japanese shapes and reinvented them. In the Comme des Garçons Autumn/Winter 1983 collection, a garter-stitch sweater owes much to the kimono, and in fact, when the wearer stretches out her arms, this effect is realized. Deceptively simple in construction, with one straight-line panel, this sweater typifies the slightly "undone" Comme look, along with the signature "face shielding" turtlenecks.

Another important deconstructionist to emerge from the 1980s, but belonging more to the avant-garde generation of the 1990s, is Martin Margiela (b.1959). Since founding the Maison Martin Margiela in 1988, the Belgian designer has been synonymous with fashion-forward contemporary knitwear. Margiela turned knit inside out, continuing the work that Sonia Rykiel had started twenty-five to thirty years earlier, but typically he twisted it in a new direction. His Spring/Summer collection of 1996 demonstrates the revolutionary way in which he reassessed knitwear: a fine-knit cardigan and pullover has been photographically printed over with a print of another knit. Thus the wearer is presented with a purposefully challenging garment—one that feels like one knit and looks like another.[5] This dissonance is an innovative way of looking at knit as a medium, challenging with intelligent, specifically dissonant concepts. In his

Autumn/Winter collection of 1999, Margiela introduced knitted shoe covers that protect the surface of each shoe so that they look brand new every time the covers are removed. Here, he suggests that something, if cared for properly, will last for a very long time.[6] His ability to constantly reposition our expectations is a fresh approach to looking at knitwear and enormously inspirational to young knitwear designers.

The 1990s saw some hugely innovative approaches to knit. The most avant-garde of the designers to emerge as the bright young things of the 1990s, along with Margiela and Alexander McQueen, is Hussein Chalayan (b.1970). His knitwear designs, much like Margiela's, are carefully considered, intelligent experiments in design. His Autumn/Winter 1998 *Scent of Tempests* collection saw Chalayan play with political taboo, and the issues of transparency first explored in the 1960s, by half covering the face in the style of a burka. This was purposefully provocative and demonstrates the blurring of the line between fashion and art.[7] Chalayan's Autumn/Winter 2006/07 collection featured a twisted black cardigan, finely fitted, with a ribbed khaki collar threaded ingeniously over the shoulders and down into the bodice, as if it were strapwork. Chalayan has recently collaborated on commercial collections with TSE knitwear.

The New York scene of the 1990s and moving into today, is well worth mentioning. Isaac Mizrahi (b.1961) and Marc Jacobs (b.1964) are the two most important figures in knitwear. Both held positions at Perry Ellis, the American label typified by its relaxed "sportswear" feel, before pursuing their own design careers. This sense of being relaxed in your clothes, at ease whilst looking smart, translated to both designers' aesthetics.

Isaac Mizrahi is a prime example of a smart "relaxed American" look, developed from the late 1980s, but a look that Mizrahi made clean and

4. Black, Sandy; *Knitwear in Fashion*, Thames and Hudson, 2002, p.37 **5.** *Fashion, The Collection of the Kyoto Costume Institute: A History from the 18th to the 20th Century*, Taschen, 2002, p.677 **6.** Ibid, p.678 **7.** Black, Sandy; *Knitwear in Fashion*, Thames and Hudson, 2002, p.105 **7.** Ibid, p.105

The "sweater girl" look, originally popular in the 1950s, has resounded through fashion up through today, being reinvented for fashion movements in new decades.

modern. His Fall 2007 ready-to-wear collection contained some pieces of relaxed women's knits—a long-sleeved jersey dress with sequin detail on the cuff, designed as if it were a T-shirt.

Marc Jacobs is perhaps the quiet man of New York fashion. His knits tend towards muted colors and he is returning to a more elegant silhouette. In the 1990s, having left Ellis, he was the leading exponent of the "grunge" movement—clothes that, though often expensive, were meant to appear old or understated. Though at first written off as quirky, he was soon seen as unconventionally cool. This culminated with a contract to design Vuitton's ready-to-wear in 1997, which he still holds.

Jacobs' first sweater, the "happy face," a club-kid sweater that he sold to Charivari (a boutique in New York), is remembered by one of Weardowney's knitters, Stacey Offer. Stacey met Marc when she was 13 in a kid's nightclub in upstate New York and they became friends. She remembers Marc's grandmother being with him, always knitting. Later, while Stacey was a student, Marc introduced her casually to Andy Warhol and the creative crowds at Studio 54. Marc's grandmother's constant knitting combined with the club kid lifestyle is what Stacey believes inspired the "happy face" and moved him into knit. Indeed, Jacobs has said that his grandmother taught him to knit and the oversized hand-knit sweaters he produced at the very beginning of his career are both domestic in flavor and nonchalantly baggy enough to be street. Jacobs has now returned to a simple, sportier, relaxed aesthetic in his knitwear, though it retains an element of dressed-down luxury.

Technology

When we think of knitting, be it machine or hand knit, the automatic assumption is that the fabric created must be for a garment or accessory. However, this ignores the countless applications the medium has. Knitting has an advantage over many textiles and fabrics in terms of its potential for strength and flexibility. As it develops technically in one area, the application for another opens up further doors. The development of engineered knit has been current since the 1960s but it is now, more than ever, that we are seeing progress in areas such as medicine and architecture, alongside the continuing innovations in art and interiors.

In terms of knit as an art form, the point at which a garment becomes an artwork is increasingly blurred. The avant-garde of the 1980s and 1990s, with designers such as Bodymap and Comme des Garçons and the more extreme fashion of Hussein Chalayan, brought fashion out of the shadows and into the realms of high art. Issey Miyake (b.1938), though less of a protagonist of hand knit, did make some interesting and technologically important advances in the field. One of the most significant is A-POC (meaning "A-Piece of Cloth"). It follows his philosophy of extracting the maximum benefits from a piece of material with minimum wastage—an eco-friendly concept.[1] Miyake introduced it to his studio in 1970 and it has no after-knitting process at all; everything is cut from one large roll of cloth, similar to the construction of the kimono—the principle of the garment being ancient but the execution being very contemporary. It is a demonstration of mass production on a grand scale, but with precision cutting, as the manufacture is computer controlled and thus retains the ability to be made to order. This single garment technology is constantly being improved but Miyake still remains at the cutting edge.

Knit certainly moved into interiors with ease. Catherine Tough is synonymous with knitted homewares. Tough, whose interiors accessories company was launched in 2000, takes traditional knit and patterns and applies them to everyday objects. She uses luxurious yarn—fine lambswool and cashmere, mainly—and her niche in luxury accessories is respected, ranging from shaped pillows to the humor of her lavender ducks and hot-water bottles with muted graphic prints.

The Italian knitwear house Missoni introduced a line of their own homewares ranging from towels to plates, pillows to throws with their signature bold prints. They have been popular, but are a product of the graphic look of Missoni rather than an innovation in knit. Cashmere is the staple of luxury knitted homewares, available from many designers, and from Loro Piana to Hermes, cashmere throws are an essential part of any home collection.

When art meets design truly original knit can happen. One of the most interesting pieces of contemporary interior design knit is the "bag" light by Lisa Gatherar (2001).[2] It is knitted from silicon rope and is a simple but highly innovative piece of contemporary design. It is not "styled" but very much design led. The light plays with the knitted texture, shining through to create a gentle glow and animating the knit.

The marriage of knitting and architecture is perhaps unexpected, but one that is proving to be most successful. The benefits are in two areas: the first is the application of knitting to scale models, and the second is the application of knitting to actual materials used.

---

1. Black, Sandy; *Knitwear in Fashion*, Thames and Hudson, 2002, p.120   2. Ibid, p.171

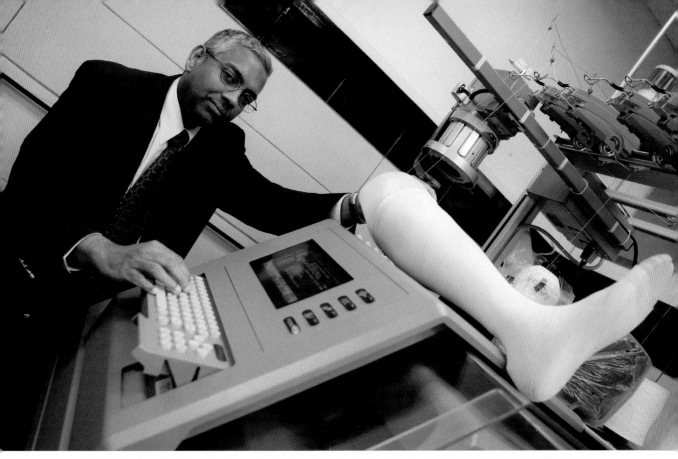

Dr. Tilak Dias from the William Lee Innovation Centre with a stocking produced using the Scan2Knit system. Photograph courtesy of Ed Swinden/The University of Manchester.

Knitting has become a key aid to those architects who have tried it for modeling purposes. Contemporary architecture is moving away from the rigid angular shapes that so defined the modernist buildings of the 1960s and 1970s and thus away from angular cardboard models. The Swiss Re building (2004) in the City of London (known as "the gherkin") and the new City Hall (2002), both designed by Lord Foster, are examples of buildings that engage new curvatures in glass and steel and that are hard to represent on a boxed-form model.

Knitted models, as unusual (and to some, no doubt, as comic) as they might sound, are proving to be highly effective in working through architectural problems and producing solutions. One architectural conference in Copenhagen is now so fascinated by knit's possibilities that

demand for knitting lessons among delegates has massively increased with each conference. Not only do the knitted models allow for flexibility in exploring form, but also give some sense of the more fluid properties that many buildings now contain. An ability to demonstrate, even if roughly, the properties a building might have in, for example, an earthquake, is of great benefit.

Knit's ability to mimic form enables it to represent a whole manner of different behaviors. Perhaps more importantly, it sows the seed for knit to be explored as a concept in architecture, the catalyst for how problems could be solved with knitted building materials.

This way of thinking was demonstrated on a rather grand scale at the 2006 London Architecture Biennale, where a group of London designers and

First knitted house in Clerkenwell during the London Architecture Biennale.

architects from The Knitting Site erected a two-story knitted house. They knitted the walls out of garbage bags, old plastic bags, and rope—things you would find on a building site. One of their aims was to start "playing with established assumptions about building sites. And houses. And knitting."[3] Their eventual statement was not ecologically driven but very much a comment on design: "Some people think that the act of building should be hidden behind screens, we like building site stuff—nets and ropes and scaffolding. We knit with them. And while some people think knitting is to remain behind walls, we build walls that are knitted."

In real-scale building, knit materials are proving to have properties that are both useful and advantageous over traditional materials. A report from the National Textile Center quotes: "Currently in the industry, woven or warp knitted coated fabrics are being used in membrane structures. The primary requirements for these structures are tensile properties, shear modulus, tear resistance, burst strength, and weatherability."[4] They discuss the fabrics they are to investigate and, while the results are of interest, it is the thought of using knit in architecture that is most interesting to us.

They explain that knitted fabrics "were designed to be lighter…allow[ing] more flexible design of architectural structures. We have chosen to explore knitted fabrics because they are relatively unknown to the industry and thus require further investigation. Knit fabrics are also highly extensible fabrics…However, these fabrics are very intriguing for architectural applications because they can be manipulated to create shapes that cannot be reproduced by woven fabrics." Again, as in fashion textiles, the three-dimensionality of knit triumphs over two-dimensional woven fabric, which, as in garment manufacture, has to be panelled and assembled. Not only do knitted fabrics have qualities of shape and reduced weight, but also strength, and they can be formed to be fire-retardant or waterproof. These knitted composites were something NASA looked into as early as the 1960s (seen in the Apollo liquid cooling garment).

The incredible strength of some of these knit and laminate composites can be remarkable. The most modern of them are now being used in boats (for hulls), as the strength and flexibility is matched by the ability to manufacture pieces on a vast scale. Knitted composites are quite standard in aviation now, as the composites' properties of lightness and flexibility are important in the fluctuating conditions exacted upon the material in the air. However, if you look at the styling of these pieces, they do have simulated rivets and other cosmetic enhancements, because to many the thought of flying in a knitted airplane is not a comforting one. This demonstrates how a

---

3. www.knittingsite.org **4**. www.ntcresearch.org, 2001

re-evaluation of the capabilities of knitting is still needed, as the common misconception of knitting as traditional and not of serious value works against most people getting used to the idea of putting faith in knitted materials.

The ecological benefits of composite knits are also being exploited. "Geo-textiles" are more in the realm of landscape architecture but their utilization of knit has proved enormously successful. Along with the benefits of creating knitted meshes to hold back geological events such as landslides, knit is also being applied to pipes and infrastructure construction.

The American Society for Testing and Materials Standards (ASTM) ruled in 2001 that "subsurface perforated drain pipes" were to be "wrapped with circular-knit geo-textile fabric to prevent them from filling with sand or sediment. A cost and time saver used in golf courses, highways, and agricultural fields, circular-knit geo-textile is applied to pipes, eliminating the need to wrap an entire trench."[5] Though this fabric had been in existence for twenty-five years previous to the ruling, it has proved its properties to the extent that it is now industry standard. That use of circular knit is a classic example of industry and the machine copying the techniques of hand knitting.

Knitting hasn't just been adapted for industrial and engineering purposes. Medical science has also benefited hugely. Medical textiles are an enormous growth area and, like architects, medics have been keen to exploit the properties that knitted textiles offer. In 2004 research at the Saint Louis University School of Medicine tested a knitted "jacket" for the heart.[6] People with moderate to severe heart failure suffer from their hearts expanding. The "CorCap Cardiac Support Device" is slipped around the heart during surgery and stitched into place. The "jacket" is mesh-like, made from a custom-knitted polyester fabric, and physically stops the heart from expanding.

Other medical knits have been successful, too, from heart valves—little meshes placed inside the arteries which open and ease blood flow—to the British "Scan2Knit" system, which knits made-to-measure compression stockings (designed to prevent venous diseases such as leg ulcers, they perhaps may be used to prevent deep vein thrombosis), developed at the William Lee Innovation Centre (part of the University of Manchester's School of Materials) in 2006.[7] There has even been a successful technique to regrow a collarbone by using a fine knit mesh of titanium on which to grow the bone.

The University of Manchester has been particularly active in the progression of knit and technology and at the beginning of 2007 it announced the development of a knitted electronic glove that remotely controls equipment via a Bluetooth connection.[8] The glove is made of acrylic and looks like a normal glove, but it has conductive pathways knitted into the material. Although commercially it is hoped to be successful in the electronic gaming industry, it has possible medical benefits for the rehabilitation of stroke victims (to monitor progress of movement achieved), and people who are wheelchair or bed bound could use the glove as a sort of remote control wired into the house to control household objects. Along with this, it has been suggested that industry might benefit from the technology, with possibilities for heating gloves through the knitted elements for those who, for example, work in refrigeration.

Other possibilities for highly advanced knitted fabrics exist too—ballistics are another growth area. Working on the principle that it is a very fine knitted version of medieval chain mail, the modern bulletproof vest often is made from an anti-ballistic knitted material, effective due to its strength. Knitted fabrics are also being tested for their soundproofing properties—it would seem that knit is truly all around us.

5. http://www.astm.org/SNEWS/NOVEMBER_2001/geotext_nov01.html   6. http://www.medicalnewstoday.com/medicalnews.php?newsid=16213
7. http://www.medicalnewstoday.com/medicalnews.php?newsid=41801   8. http://www.theengineer.co.uk/Articles/298394/EFS+points+to+the+future.htm

Knit Today

Though many established names are doing interesting and worthwhile things with hand and machine knit, a few select designers are really pushing the medium forward.

Julian MacDonald is one of Britain's most established and celebrated contemporary designers. Before launching his label in 1997, the Welsh designer was enormously interested in knitwear, learning the craft from his mother and refining it designing knitwear at Chanel for Karl Lagerfeld and then for Alexander McQueen. It was while at Chanel that he first pushed the boundaries of the abilities of knit as a medium, knitting sterling silver pieces.

MacDonald's knitwear designs in the 1990s were hand knits that were both highly fragile and technically accomplished. He became known for his "cobweb" knits, made up into bright-green lurex crocheted minidresses.[1] His graduate collection (1996) first featured these cobweb knits and his dresses were entire confections of fantasy. In later collections he used beading and sequins, developing an emphasis on glamour and a re-invigorated sexuality that his name has become synonymous with. Later experiments with metallic yarn continued MacDonald's exploration of high-glamour knitwear and, after a break in 2005, he returned to knit with pearl-embroidered cardigans.

Alex Gore Browne has found success since graduating in knitwear from Central Saint Martins School of Art in London. Her delicate knits have been seen on everyone from Madonna to Kate Moss, and have received good critical reception with *Vogue* magazine describing her first venture into daywear as "no one-knit wonder." Having learned to knit at her grandmother's knee—her first piece of fashion design was a knitted purse with a button in the middle—she rediscovered knit

---

1. McDermott, Catherine; *Made in Britain*, Octopus, 2002

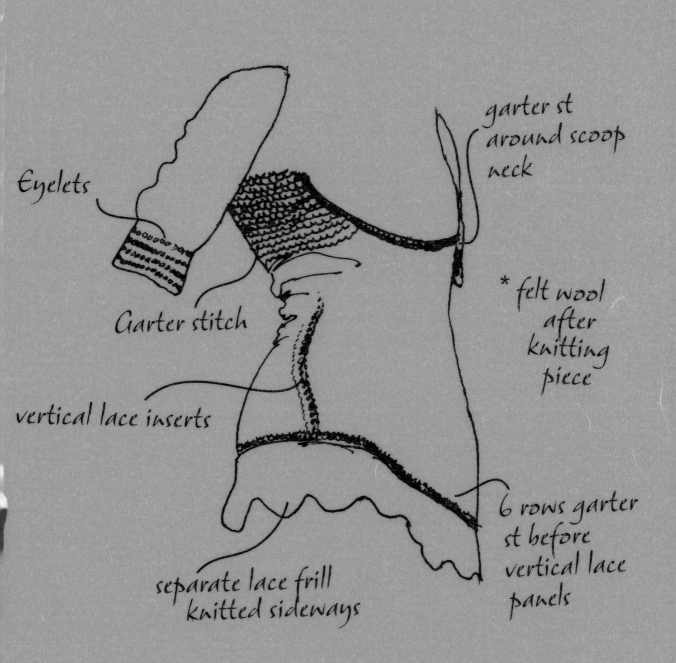

Eyelets

Garter stitch

garter st
around scoop
neck

* felt wool
after
knitting
piece

vertical lace inserts

6 rows garter
st before
vertical lace
panels

separate lace frill
knitted sideways

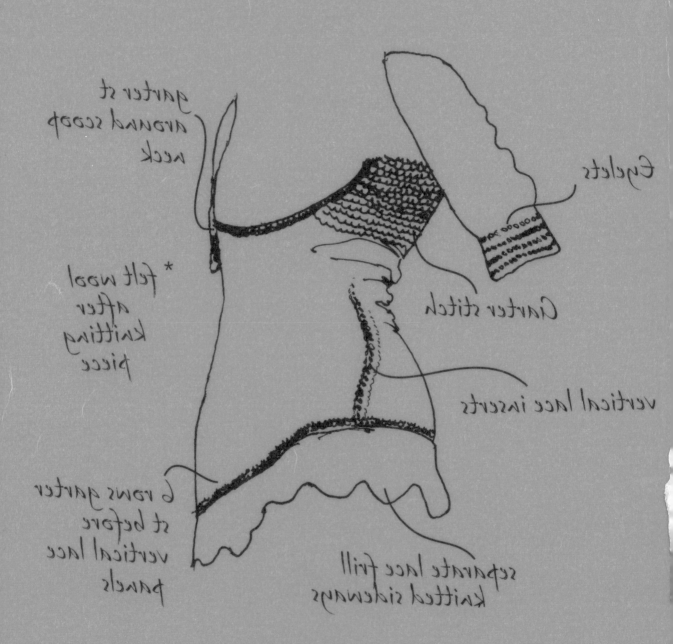

Philip Colbert and Richard Ascott of Rodnik show off a cardigan made from their signature "pookh" material.

as a medium at age nineteen. Textile students tend to bifurcate into those who are interested in print and those who are interested in structured textiles—Gore Browne turned to the latter.

Her signature knits focus on a lightness of material (mainly cashmere and merino wool) and structure. "I love the way you can be architectural with knit," she explains, and her approach to determining silhouette is, in her own terms, all about "sculpting." What makes her a knitwear designer, rather than stylist, is the way in which she treats the medium. Gore Browne is led by "the characteristics in a fabric to create garment shape." A signature detail is little flared elements that make the knit kick out. She achieves this by pulling the stitching in, designing the knit so that it is the fabric that will create the effect—thus "the fabric controls the garment."

Creating unusual textures through delicate structure is more difficult in commercial collections, and the British label Ghost has recently taken on Gore Browne to design a range of knitwear. Again, she makes sure that the fabric, and its quality, leads the design but in a more restrained manner than in her own line. She refuses to imitate other brands, ensuring that commercial collaboration can retain originality in design and not simply ape the catwalk.

In terms of where knit is going, Gore Browne believes that "slinky," fine-gauge knits are set to become even more popular, partly due to the inherent versatility of the fabric. She believes in the wearability of knit and its ability to add structure to a garment, even if the material is essentially two-dimensional. Flatness, with which we associate fine-gauge knit, is not necessarily "flat" in the way a garment is constructed. Her starting point is always the body, and the way in which the designer is able to "wrap lines around it," binding it with a more natural shape.

Gore Browne also experiments with adding texture to fine-gauge knit. Her Autumn/Winter 2005 collection incorporated leather sequins into jersey. The large, gold-printed leather disks overlap to create scallop effects on the sleeves. They provide not only textural interest but also modern, elegant lines and a graphic quality created by sculpting the knit. She proves that the capabilities of the advance of knitted form are vast, even for flat knitted material.

Clare Tough is another Saint Martins knitwear graduate who has found success in bringing attention to knitwear on the London fashion scene. Described by *Vogue* as "the future of British fashion," her collection was snapped up by Browns boutique and the Regent Street store Liberty, in London. She has shown proficiency in moving the ideas of traditional knit forward through championing constructed textiles. She mixes techniques, from hand to machine knit and crochet, as well as developing entirely new ideas, such as knitting chain with yarn.

Tough's Autumn/Winter 2006 collection had oversized jumpers and vests with gold chains alongside body-conscious tightness and corsetry. Clearly inspired by the natural female form, she "sexed-up" knitwear with these corsetry effects, using stitched lurex circles around the bust to create an exaggerated silhouette.

Rodnik is a label that has had the fashion press buzzing in both the UK and the USA. Having caught the attention of the editor-in-chief of American *Vogue*, Anna Wintour, and having been taken under the wing of Chanel's current master, Karl Lagerfeld, the label can only continue to ascend with understated fervor. They already count actresses Lauren Bacall, Scarlett Johansson, and Sienna Miller, as well as Queen Rania of Jordan and British supermodel Lily Cole as customers.

Rodnik is the brainchild of college friends Philip Colbert and Richard Ascott. Modest in their abilities, they have set about creating their own fashion characters, appearing at fashion events with small matching parasols (a version of which they presented to Lagerfeld—who then placed pink parasols on his Chanel front row for attendees in 2006), and T-shirts with drawings of themselves.

They have been stated as wishing to bridge the gap between the romance of pre-Revolution Russia and contemporary fashion, and the name "Rodnik" was inspired by the original Rodnik shop in Moscow—founded by the Russian Princess Maria Tenesheva in 1904. The name is derived from the Russian word for "the source," with the original store catering to the Russian elite. Tenesheva employed folk craftsmen, *Kustar*, with the aim of maintaining the essence of Russian fashion and culture and in doing so, the "essence of their nation."

The signature Rodnik material is "Pookh," a fabric created from the gruff of a breed of mountain

Pringle is just one of the established knitwear labels creating new knit looks today.

goat found in the foothills of the Urals. Their combination of other fabrics with this cobwebbed knit drives the contemporary appeal of their designs. Pookh is hand knitted in Russia and then cut and sewn into garments in the London studio. Because of the material's fragility the knit is not made up into fully fashioned knitted garments, but rather Rodink designs around this base material.

They admit to the natural limitations of the knit itself, but are developing it in directions that are unexpected from such a tradition. Developing and changing their direction is key to each new season and each collection features a variant design on a folk pattern. One such development will feature their own faces—taking on an almost Schiaparelli quality in introducing the surrealist touch of integrating their images into the pattern. They are also experimenting with crochet, refining the

Lowie's matinee jacket from the Summer 2007 collection.

delicacy of fine-gauge, complex patterns to adapt them into delicate crochet dresses.

The Rodnik Spring/Summer collection of 2007 contains mixed use of knit. Alongside combinations of Pookh with jersey—layering on details reminiscent of Victorian lace edging—Rodnik team tailored jersey dresses printed with lace knit and worn with Pookh cardigans and capes with coordinating satin edging. Accessories such as hats and signature shawls and scarves all carry the Pookh material in one form or another. Overall the collections feel ethereal and delicately feminine. The Victoriana is developing into post-modern iconic "rock knit" (as they describe it), and certainly lives up to their tongue-in-cheek description of Rodnik as a "woolly-mix."

London is somewhat of a nucleus in knit revolution at present. Another new generation hand-knit designer is Bronwyn Lowenthal, who launched the Lowie label in 2003. When the first collection of hand-knit accessories appeared, Urban Outfitters and UK department store House of Fraser quickly snapped it up.

Pieces are handcrafted and employ crochet, hand embroidery and hand stitching alongside hand knitting. Very much in tune with the ethos of Weardowney, the label is ethically driven, providing handcrafted items at reasonable prices for which the craftsmen involved in their production have been fairly compensated. The label is now stocked in stores all around the world, including Australia, Taiwan, and Japan, and represents the ever-increasing consumer appreciation of true craftsmanship in fashion today.

Lowie describes itself as appealing to "women who appreciate handicrafts and good fun fashion," and emphasize that "while our fashion accessories might happen to be on trend, we don't take our designs too seriously and so neither do our customers." They continue a trait in knitters and knitwear designers to be above self-absorbed gravity of purpose and, though serious about knit, they do not worry about appearing to be constantly "now"—instead being consciously "uncool."

By the nature of hand knit, each piece is individual and has its quirks and differences, attributes celebrated in the Lowie ethos. In Spring/Summer 2006, Lowie introduced cotton summer knitwear with nautical-inspired striped berets. Indeed, the beret has become a Lowie signature with Autumn/Winter 2006 incorporating a multitude of alternate styles. These included the crocheted "Left Bank" look to mohair and knitted rabbit alongside knitted cloche hats, chunky-knit berets, and flat-caps detailed with knitted flowers. Chunky zigzag-patterned snoods, virgin-wool belts, and mittens are some of the more esoteric, yet practical, accessories featured.

Britain's love of traditional knit came back "on trend" in the twenty-first century. In menswear the Argyle pattern crossed over from the stereotypical golfing uniform to symbolize nonchalant street trend. The "geek chic" that came into fashion around 2003/4 took the Argyle and applied it to fine-gauge sweaters from designer to ready-to-wear. Pringle is the best-known protagonist of the pattern and, indeed, is credited for its invention. The current trend is a reexamination of the tight Argyle popularized in the 1970s. Pringle has also led the revival of chunky knits, as seen in their Autumn/Winter collections for 2006 and 2007.

In 2007, Clare Waight Keller, the creative director of Pringle, utilized cashmere crochet and mohair cable separates to be worn over light, sharp clothes, giving texture and a feeling of cozy weight. Worth mentioning alongside the revival of chunky knit is the designer Nicole Farhi, who continues to popularize the "sloppy joe," a 1950s hand-knit revival style that she has kept throughout the 1990s through to today.

Giles Deacon showed knit in a bombastic light in his Autumn/Winter 2007 collection. His treatment of knit moved from the metallic and pearlized dipped knit from the year before to a gargantuan take on the cable-knit sweater. It was even described as the first time a "sea cucumber" had been used for inspiration in a catwalk show. The new large knits are hand worked, but the scale is almost industrial and is applied to belted cardigans (twice the size of the models wearing them), scarves, and hooded short-waist sweaters.

Celebrity knitting

The domestic knitting scene has never been more active in both the UK and the USA. Knitting has taken on a new "cool" and is moving away from its previous overtones of domestic drudgery, woolly 1970s craft movements, and old-fashioned, more "senior" associations. Instead, it has come out of the craft closet and has emerged as a fashionable pastime. This seems due to a number of contributing factors, namely the need for escape in busy modern working life, the cult of self-help and therapy, nostalgia and the popularity of "vintage," and the rise of celebrity knitting.

Celebrities knitting have become a regular sight in gossip magazines. Many Hollywood stars have been photographed on set and relaxing while working away with their needles. Julia Roberts is the most often mentioned, but we must add Madonna, Hilary Swank, Cameron Diaz, Sandra Bullock, Daryl Hannah, Goldie Hawn, Julianne Moore, Sarah-Jessica Parker, and Kate Moss to the list, along with celebrity couples such as Courtney Cox and David Arquette, Jennifer Aniston and Brad Pitt (when they were still together), and, perhaps most surprisingly, actor Russell Crowe and his wife.[2]

An extraordinary paper was published in 2004 entitled *Celebrity Knitting and the Temporality of Postmodernity* by Wendy Parkins, in which she explored all the aspects of why celebrities knit and the relevance it has for us today. She set out the reasons for the existence of a new wave of younger

knitters and clarified the benefits celebrity knitters get from knitting, and in turn the benefits that knitting has received.

One of Parkins' conclusions as to why knitting has become so popular with celebrities is the idea of "ordinary performance." As the reading public's hunger for snapshots of celebrities in their natural habitat grows, pictures of them knitting show us the celebrity involved in a domestic activity normally associated with the home and the "private" sphere. As Parkins explains: "The knitting celebrity becomes endowed with the qualities of ordinariness and authenticity and hence enhances their appeal; while celebrity knitting lends a public face, a youthful aura and a glamour to knitting."[3] This is the most straightforward explanation, but Parkins continues by going into other areas that uncover knitting as relevant for the modern world.

The first is a sense of time in an increasingly hectic world: "While speed is often seen as the defining feature of (post) modern society, it is the acceleration of processes, especially of transport and communication, that makes an awareness of slowness possible." She sees knitting as time for the self, "an alternative temporality, defined against the acceleration of other areas of life", and part of a more nostalgic movement that equates the good life with a slow life. The second area is the attempt at a new domestic femininity, citing Nigella Lawson as the perfect example of the new "post feminist," and explains knitting as a post-modern, post-feminist activity: "Knitting is here represented as a source of pleasure and connectedness for time-pressured women."

The third and final validation of the relevance of knitting today is its spiritual, or therapeutic, qualities. Here Parkins talks about "zen" knitting— the idea that knitting can be meditative in practice with time to "remake the self," and mentions the Hollywood actress Daryl Hannah as the most well known practitioner of "zen" knitting. Indeed, Susan

---

2. Parkins, Wendy; *Celebrity Knitting and the Temporality of Postmodernity*, Fashion Theory, vol. 8, issue 4, 2004, p.425   3. Ibid. p.431

Lydon's popular 1997 publication, *The Knitting Sutra: Craft as a Spiritual Practice*, points to pace, rhythms, and historicity—an extension of slow knitting, as it were.

Parkins has some interesting points, though citing knitting as a feminist pursuit is perhaps taking it a little further than necessary. Certainly, the rhythmic quality of knitting could be construed as meditative and there is indeed a cult of the "self" in today's urban population. Whether it will remain a fad among celebrities, who knows. By the nature of performing arts there is a lot of waiting around and many people have, and do, pass the time by knitting. Certainly the craft looks like it won't disappear from contemporary fashion for now. And its presence on the Internet is certainly most astounding.

Knitting on the net

Knitters, by definition, tend towards community and, with the development of the Internet, communities have transferred from drawing rooms, sitting rooms, and church halls into cyberspace. There is an enormous number of websites devoted to knitting—some useful, others misleading. With the numerous events available there will always be a place to meet and improve technique with others. Names like "knit n natter," "stitch n bitch," and "knit happens," suggest a light-hearted look at things in this new lexicon of knit. The wonderful blog entitled "You knit what? Seriously. What the hell were you thinking?", in which the author throws a barrage of abuse at the reader, and "the knitting curmudgeon," who also swears liberally, are typical of the new breed of online knitting communities that don't take themselves too seriously.

Guerrilla knitters are one of the more unusual communities to emerge on the Internet. Some are "political" knitters, believing the craft to represent an act of rebellion. Shane Waltener, an artist,

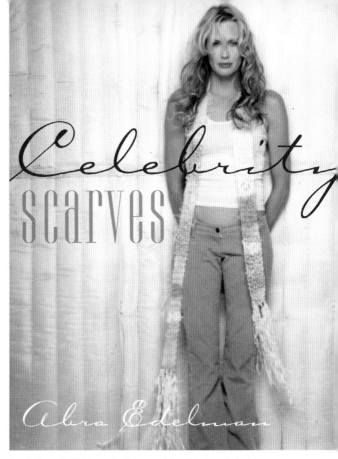

Daryl Hannah, Hollywood actress and "zen" knitter, is just one of today's knitting celebrities.

specializes in this type of knit. "By knitting you are resisting capitalism and consumerism. You are not responding to the fashion industry; you are making your own decisions."[4] Cast Off is a club that even stages knit-ins on the London Underground, occupying a carriage and knitting around the Circle line, and was once ejected from the Savoy Hotel in London for refusing to stop knitting.[5] Such extremes were even celebrated in a Crafts Council exhibition on extreme knitted forms in 2005, *Knit 2 together*, at which time they released a new pattern for a "grenade purse."

Knitting is alive and well in popular culture, through celebrities, new, younger audiences, and the Internet. The craft has been reborn with established and new designers using knit in a way that pushes it forward as a medium into new and interesting areas.

---

4. http://www.we-make-money-not-art.com/archives/004323.php **5.** www.castoff.info

Knitting the projects

The basics of knitting are best-learned hands on—with another knitter at your side—by doing, undoing, and seeing what and why. Though learning from books is useful, knitting classes are well worth attending and are increasingly available, so do look for one near you.

In tackling the knitting projects in this book, your approach should always be one of making your own design choices at each stage of the work. Shape, color, yarn texture, handle, stitch pattern, and color arrangement can all be looked at separately when you select a particular project. They can then be combined as you wish to determine the overall personality of the style you make. This will result in a garment that means much more to you—its maker—than simply owning or gifting a garment you have made following someone else's taste.

The Peacock Skirt on page 86, for instance, was inspired by a petticoat I once saw in the Victoria and Albert Museum. Over two yards in width and knitted in the round, this was an unfinished knitting masterpiece that had a self-colored jacquard pattern with virtually no repeat, so maximum concentration must have been needed for every stitch on every row. The petticoat was also worked in very fine thread, on equally fine needles, and even with today's technology this extraordinary piece could not have been worked by machine and achieved the same spectacular quality.

All the projects in this book are based around seven different shapes that, with varying yarn and stitch choices, take on entirely different characters. For example, the Spiderweb Bolero can be transformed into a casual yet flirty daytime cover-up by simply changing the stitch pattern, adding a ruffle to the edges, and embellishing it with a ribbon tie around the waist. Each project has a difficulty level indicated by one to three balls of yarn at the top of the page. A single ball indicates a project a beginner could try, while three balls tells you the project is for experienced knitters.

Creating your own designs is a very fun and rewarding process, so feel free to experiment and remember—practice makes perfect!

Gail Downey

Spiderweb Bolero

SIZE
Small:medium:large
Bust 34:36:38in
Length 14¾:17⅝:20⅜in
Sleeve 14⅜:14⅜:14⅜in

YARN
Twilleys Goldfingering in 1¾oz (50g) balls (80% viscose/20% polyester), approx 200yd (200m)

4(4:4) x Ebony 31

NEEDLES
Pair of US 3 needles

GAUGE
1 pattern repeat (6 sts) measures 1in wide; 3 pattern repeats (18 rows) measure 4in high.

ABBREVIATIONS
See page 142.

SPECIAL NOTE
Spiderweb pattern
Row 1: K1, * P5tog, [K1, P1, K1, P1, K1] into next st before slipping it off needle, rep from * to last st, K1.
Rows 2 and 4: Purl.
Row 3: K1, * [K1, P1, K1, P1, K1] into next st, P5tog, rep from * to last st, K1.
Row 5: [Insert needle knitwise into 1st st, yon 3 times then knit st] into every stitch.
Row 6: [Knit 1st loop of the yon and drop the other 2] into every st (so returning to original stitch count).

BACK
With US 3 needles, cast on 104(110:116) sts.
Work 5(6:7) spiderweb patt reps.
Work 4 rows of next patt rep.
Armhole shaping
Bind off 6 sts at beg of next 2 rows. *92(98:104) sts*
Cont without shaping until 11(13:15) patts and 4 rows of next patt rep have been completed.
Bind off.

LEFT FRONT
With US 3 needles, cast on 56(62:68) sts.
Work 5(6:7) spider web patt reps.
Work 4 rows of next patt rep. **
Armhole shaping
Next row (RS) (5th row of patt): Bind off 6 sts, patt to end. *50(56:62) sts*
Cont without shaping until 9(11:13) patts and 3 rows of next patt rep have been completed.
Neck shaping
Next row (WS) (4th row of patt): Bind off 12 sts, patt to end.
Patt 7 rows.

Next row (WS) (6th row of patt): Bind off 6 sts, patt to end. *32(38:44) sts*
Patt 3 rows, so ending with 3rd row of 12th(14th:16th) patt rep.
Bind off.

RIGHT FRONT
Work as for Left Front to **.
Patt 1 row.
Armhole shaping
Next row (WS) (6th row of patt): Bind off 6 sts, patt to end. *50(56:62) sts*
Cont without shaping until 9(11:13) patts and 4 rows of next patt rep have been completed.
Neck shaping
Next row (RS) (5th row of patt): Bind off 12 sts, patt to end.
Work 7 rows of patt.
Next row (RS) (1st row of patt): Bind off 6 sts, patt to end. *32(38:44) sts*
Patt 2 rows, so ending with 3rd row of 12th(14th:16th) patt rep.
Bind off.

SLEEVES

With US 3 needles, cast on 74 sts.

Work 11 patt reps.

Work 4 rows of next patt rep.

Armhole shaping

Bind off 6 sts at beg of next
2 rows. *62 sts*

Work without shaping until 13 patt
reps and 4 rows of 14th patt rep
have been completed.

Bind off.

FOR THE TIES

(make two)

With US 3 needles, cast on 6 sts.

Patt row: Slip 1 st, K5.

Rep the patt row until tie measures
12in long.

Bind off.

FINISHING

Join shoulder seams, matching
stitches. Sew sleeves into
armholes. Join side and sleeve
seams. Sew ties to front edges.

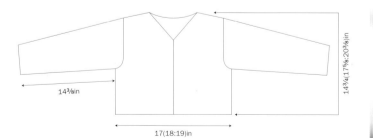

14³⁄₈in

17(18:19)in

14³⁄₄(17⁵⁄₈:20³⁄₈)in

Lace and Ribbon Bolero

SIZE

Small:medium:large
Bust 43¼:46⅜:49⅝in
Length 13⅝:15¼:17¼in
Sleeve 4⅞in

YARN

RYC Bamboo Soft in 1¾oz (50g)
balls (100% bamboo), approx 82yd
(75m)
  8(9:10) x Gypsum 111
1⅝yd of satin ribbon

NEEDLES

Pair of US 3 needles
US 3 16in-long circular needle

GAUGE

20 sts and 36 rows to 4in over lace
patt using US 3 needles

ABBREVIATIONS

See page 142.

SPECIAL NOTE

Lace pattern

Row 1 (RS): * Yfwd, sl1, K1, psso,
rep from * to end.
Row 2: Knit.
Row 3: * Yfwd, K2tog, rep from *
to end.

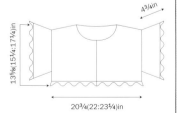

13⅝(15¼:17¼)in

4¾in

20¾(22:23¼)in

BACK

Using US 3 needles, cast on
208(220:232) sts
Rows 1–6: Knit.
Row 7: * K2tog, rep from * to end.
104(110:116) sts
Rows 8–19: Knit.
Work 6(7:8) lace patt reps.
Work 4 rows of 7th(8th:9th) rep.
Armhole shaping
Bind off 6 sts at beg of next
2 rows. *92(98:104) sts*
Cont without shaping until
13(15:17) patt reps and 4 rows of
14th(16th:18th) rep completed.
Bind off.

LEFT FRONT

Using US 3 needles, cast on
112(122:132) sts.
Rows 1–6: Knit.
Row 7: * K2tog, rep from * to end.
56(61:66) sts
Rows 8–19: Knit.
Work 6(7:8) lace patt reps.
Work 4 rows of 7th(8th:9th) rep. **
Armhole shaping
Next row (RS): Bind off 6 sts, patt
to end. *50(55:60) sts*
Cont without shaping until
11(13:15) patt reps and 5 rows of
12th(14th:16th) rep completed.
Neck shaping
Next row (WS): Bind off 18 sts, patt
to end.
Cont without shaping until
13(15:17) patt reps and 4 rows of
14th(16th:18th) rep completed.
Bind off.

RIGHT FRONT

Work as for Left Front to **, then
patt 1 more row.
Armhole shaping
Next row: Bind off 6 sts, patt to end.
Cont without shaping until
11(13:15) patt reps and 4 rows of
12th(14th:16th) rep completed.
Neck shaping
Next row: Bind off 18 sts, patt to end.
Cont without shaping until
13(15:17) patts and 4 rows of
14th(16th:18th) rep completed.
Bind off.

FINISHING

Join side and shoulder seams.
Thread ribbon through eyelets at
waist to tie in front.

SLEEVES

Using US 3 circular needle and
starting at the bottom, pick up
105(110:115) sts around armhole.
Place a round marker.
Round 1: Knit.
Round 2: Purl.
These 2 rounds form garter st patt.
Patt 38 more rounds.
Next round: * Insert needle knitwise
into 1st st, yon 3 times then knit
st, rep from * to end.
Next round: [Purl 1st loop of
the triple yon and drop the other
2 loops] into every st.
Work 2 more rounds in garter st.
Next round: Knit twice into every st.
Work 6 rounds in garter st.
Bind off.

Cap-Sleeve Bolero

SIZE

Small:medium:large

Bust 43¼:46⅜:49⅝in

Length 12¾:14⅜:16⅜in

Sleeve 2⅞in

YARN

RYC Bamboo Soft in 1¾oz balls
(100% bamboo), approx 82yd (75m)

   5(6:7) in Cream 100 (A)

   4(5:6) in Hemp 104 (B)

Two buttons

NEEDLES

Pair of US 3 needles

US 3 16in-long circular needle

GAUGE

20 sts and 36 rows to 4in over lace
patt using US 3 needles.

ABBREVIATIONS

See page 142.

SPECIAL NOTE

Lace pattern

Row 1 (RS): * Yfwd, sl1, K1, psso,
rep from * to end.

Rows 2 and 4–8: Knit.

Row 3: * Yfwd, K2tog, rep from *
to end.

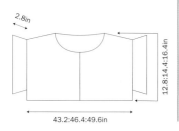

2.8in

12.8:14.4:16.4in

43.2:46.4:49.6in

BACK

Using US 3 needles and yarn B,
cast on 104(110:116) sts.

Rows 1–11: Knit.

Work 5(6:7) lace patt reps.

Change to yarn A.

Work 1 patt rep and 4 rows of
7th(8th:9th) patt rep.

Armhole shaping

Bind off 6 sts at beg of next
2 rows. *92(98:104) sts*

Cont without shaping until
13(15:17) patts and 4 rows of
14th(16th:18th) patt rep have
been completed.

Bind off.

LEFT FRONT

Using US 3 needles and yarn B,
cast on 56(61:66) sts.

Rows 1–11: Knit.

Work 5(6:7) lace patt reps.

Change to yarn A.

Work 1 patt rep and 4 rows of
7th(8th:9th) patt rep. **

Armhole shaping

Next row (RS): Bind off 6 sts, patt
to end. *50(55:60) sts*

Cont without shaping until
11(13:15) patt reps and 5 rows of
12th(14th:16th) patt rep have
been completed.

Neck shaping

Next row (WS): Bind off 18 sts, patt
to end. *32(37:42) sts*

Cont without shaping until
13(15:17) patt reps and 4 rows of
14th(16th:18th) patt rep have
been completed.

Bind off.

RIGHT FRONT

Work as for Left Front to **, then
patt 1 more row.

Armhole shaping

Next row (RS): Bind off 6 sts, patt
to end.

Cont without shaping until
11(13:15) patt reps and 4 rows of
12th(14th:16th) patt rep have
been completed.

Neck shaping

Next row (RS): Bind off 18 sts, patt
to end. *32(37:42) sts*

Cont without shaping until
13(15:17) patt reps and 4 rows of
14th(16th:18th) patt rep have
been completed.

Bind off.

FINISHING

Join side and shoulder seams. Sew
buttons to bottom of bolero fronts,
slipping them through aligning
eyelets to fasten.

SLEEVES

Using US 3 circular needle, yarn A
and starting at the bottom of the
armhole, pick up 105(110:115) sts
from around the armhole.

Place a round marker.

Round 1: Knit.

Round 2: Purl.

These 2 rounds on circular needles
form garter st patt.

Patt 30 more rounds.

Bind off.

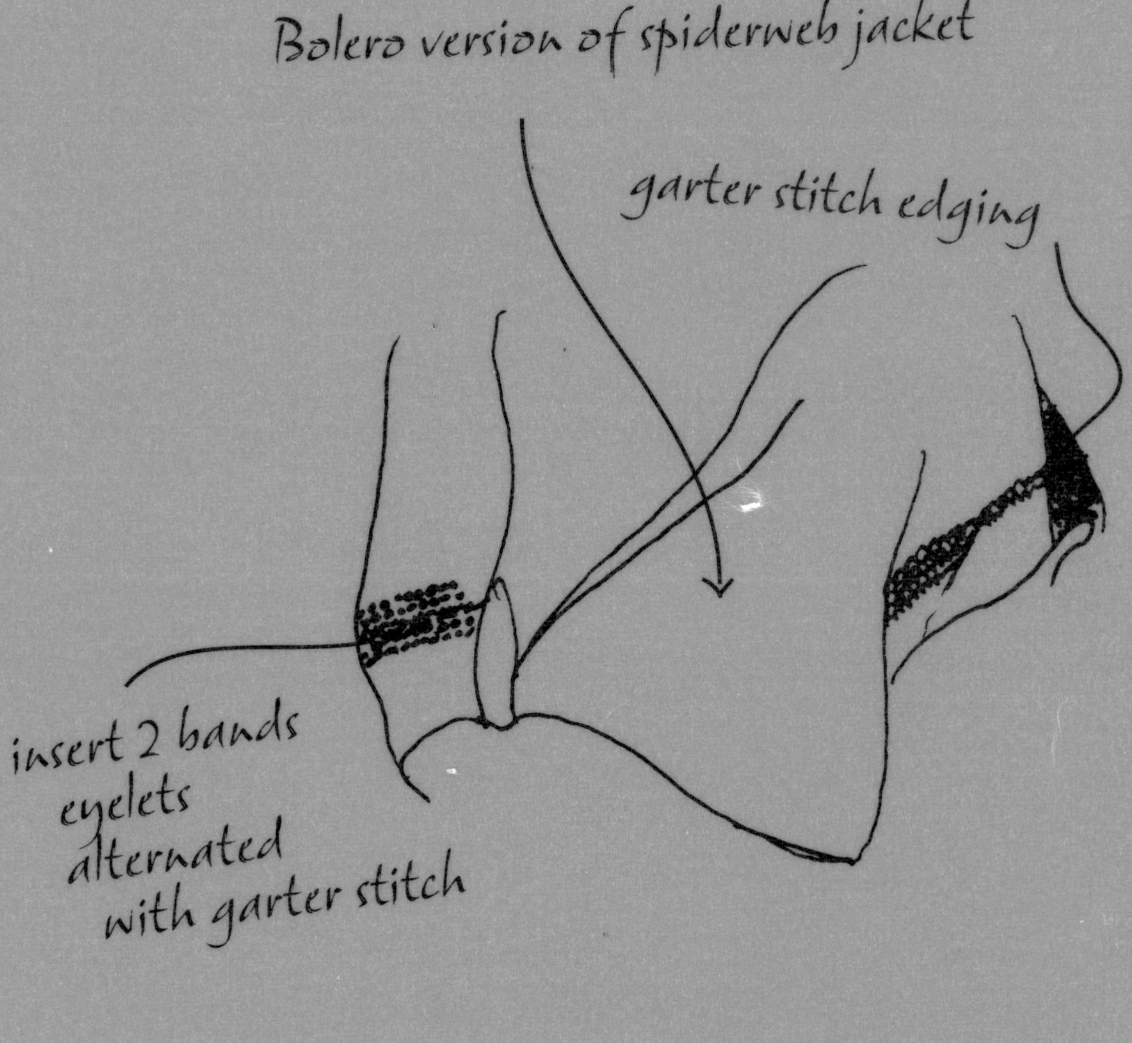

Bolero version of spiderweb jacket

garter stitch edging

insert 2 bands
eyelets
alternated
with garter stitch

Bolero version of spiderweb jacket

garter stitch edging

insert 2 bands eyelets alternated with garter stitch

Peacock Skirt

SIZE

Small:medium

Waist 30⅜:34⅜in

Length approximately 24in

YARN

Twilleys Goldfingering in 1¾oz (50g) balls (80% viscose/20% polyester), approx 218yd (200m)

7(7) x Burgundy 58

Waist length of elastic

NEEDLES

Pair of US 3 needles

US 3 32in-long circular needle

GAUGE

29 sts and 41 rows to 4in over stockinette stitch on US 3 needles.

ABBREVIATIONS

See page 142.

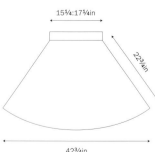

15¼:17¼in

22¾in

42¾in

SKIRT

Using US 3 needles, cast on 140(160) sts.

Row 1 (RS): * K1, P1, rep from * to end.

This row forms rib and is repeated. Work in rib for 2⅞in.

Change to US 3 circular needle. Place a marker to indicate start of rounds.

1st size only

Round 1: Knit.

Round 2: * Yfwd, K1 tbl, yfwd, K13, rep from * to end. *160 sts*

Both sizes

Round 3: [K1 tbl] in every st.

Round 4: * Yon twice, sl1, K2tog, psso, yon twice, sl1, K1, psso, K9, K2tog, rep from * to end.

Round 5 and every foll alt round: As round 3, working K1, P1 into each double yon of previous round.

Round 6: * Yfwd, K1 tbl, yon twice, sl1, K2tog, psso, yon twice, K1tbl, yfwd, sl1, K1, psso, K7, K2tog, rep from * to end. *180 sts*

Round 8: * [Yon twice, sl1, K2tog, psso] 3 times, yon twice, sl1, K1, psso, K5, K2tog, rep from * to end.

Round 10: * Yfwd, K1 tbl, [yon twice, sl1, K2tog, psso] 3 times, yon twice, K1 tbl, yfwd, sl1, K1, psso, K3, K2tog, rep from * to end. *200 sts*

Round 12: * [Yon twice, sl1, K2tog, psso] 5 times, yon twice, sl1, K1, psso, K1, K2tog, rep from * to end.

Round 14: * Yfwd, K1 tbl, [yon twice, sl, K2tog, psso] 5 times, yon twice, K1 tbl, ywfd, sl1, K2tog, psso, rep from * to end. *220 sts*

Rounds 16, 18 and 20: * Yfwd, sl1, K2tog, psso, [yon twice, sl1, K2tog, psso] 6 times, ywfd, K1 tbl, rep from * to end.

Round 21: As round 5 to last 2 sts, these 2 sts will form first 2 sts of next round.

Replace marker here to indicate new start of rounds.

Round 22: * Yfwd, K3, ywfd, sl1, K1, psso, yfwd, sl1, K2tog, psso, [yon twice, sl1, K2tog, psso] 4 times, yfwd, K2tog, rep from * to end.

Round 24: * Yfwd, K5, yfwd, sl1, K1, psso, K2tog, [yon twice, sl1, K2tog, psso] 3 times, yon twice, sl1, K1, psso, K2tog, rep from * to end.

Round 26: * Yfwd, K7, yfwd, K3tog tbl, [yon twice, sl1, K2tog, psso] 3 times, yon twice, K3tog, rep from * to end.

Round 28: * Yfwd, K9, yfwd, sl1, K1, psso, yfwd, [sl1, K2tog, psso, yon twice] twice, sl1, K2tog, psso, yfwd, K2tog, rep from * to end.

Round 30: * Yfwd, K11, yfwd, sl1, K1, psso, K2tog, yon twice, sl1, K2tog, psso, yon twice, sl1, K1, psso, K2tog, rep from * to end.

Round 32: * Yfwd, K13, yfwd, K3tog tbl, yon twice, sl1, K2tog, psso, yon twice, K3tog, rep from * to end.

Round 34: * Yfwd, K15, yfwd, sl1, K1, psso, yfwd, sl1, K2tog, psso, yfwd, K2tog, rep from * to end.

Round 36: * Yfwd, K17, yfwd, sl1, K1, psso, K1, K2tog, rep from * to end.

Round 38: * Yfwd, K19, yfwd, sl1, K2tog, psso, rep from * to end.

Round 40: * Yfwd, K21, yfwd, K1 tbl, rep from * to end. *240 sts*

Round 42: K11, replace marker here for new start of rounds, * yfwd, K1 tbl, yfwd, sl1, K1, psso, K19, K2tog, rep from * to end.

Round 44: * Yon twice, sl1, K2tog, psso, yon twice, sl1, K1, psso, K17, K2tog, rep from * to end.

Round 46: * Yfwd, K1 tbl, yon twice, sl1, K2tog, psso, yon twice, K1 tbl, yfwd, sl1, K1, psso, K15, K2tog, rep from * to end. *260 sts*

Round 48: * [Yon twice, sl1, K2tog, psso] 3 times, yon twice, sl1, K1, psso, K13, K2tog, rep from * to end.

Round 50: * Yfwd, K1 tbl, [yon twice, sl1, K2tog, psso] 3 times, yon twice, K1 tbl, yfwd, sl1, K1, psso, K11, K2tog, rep from * to end. *280 sts*

Round 52: * [Yon twice, sl1, K2tog, psso] 5 times, yon twice, sl1, K1, psso, K9, K2tog, rep from * to end.

Round 54: * Yon twice, K1 tbl, [yon twice, sl1, K2tog, psso] 5 times, yon twice, K1 tbl, yon twice, sl1, K1, psso, K7, K2tog, rep from * to end. *320 sts*

Round 56: * Yon twice, K1 tbl, [yon twice, sl1, K2tog, psso] 7 times, yon twice, K1 tbl, yon twice, sl1, K1, psso, K5, K2tog, rep from * to end. *360 sts*

Round 58: * Yon twice, K1 tbl, [yon twice, sl1, K2tog, psso] 9 times,

yon twice, K1 tbl, yon twice, sl1, K1, psso, K3, K2tog, rep from * to end. *400 sts*

Round 60: * Yon twice, K1 tbl, [yon twice, sl1, K2tog, psso] 11 times, yon twice, K1 tbl, yon twice, sl1, K1, psso, K1, K2tog, rep from * to end. *440 sts*

Round 62: * Yon twice, K1 tbl, [yon twice, sl1, K2tog, psso] 13 times, yon twice, K1 tbl, yon twice, sl1, K2tog, psso, rep from * to end. *480 sts*

Rounds 64, 66, 68 and 70: K1, * yon twice, sl1, K2tog, psso, rep from * to end.

Round 72: K1, * [yon twice, sl1, K2tog, psso] 3 times, yfwd, K1, inc into next st, K1, yfwd, sl1, K2tog, psso, [yon twice, sl1, K2tog, psso] 3 times, rep from * to end. *500 sts*

Round 74: K1, * [yon twice, sl1, K2tog, psso] 3 times, yfwd, K2tog, yfwd, sl1, K1, psso, yfwd, sl1, K2tog, psso, [yon twice, sl1, K2tog, psso] 3 times, rep from * to end. *480 sts*

Round 76: K1, * [yon twice, sl1, K2tog, psso] twice, yon twice, sl1, K1, psso, K2tog, yfwd, K1 tbl, yfwd, sl1, K1, psso, K2tog, [yon twice, sl1, K2tog, psso] 3 times, rep from * to end.

Round 78: K1, * [yon twice, sl1, K2tog, psso] twice, yon twice, K3tog, yfwd, K3, yfwd, K3tog tbl, [yon twice, sl1, K2tog, psso] 3 times, rep from * to end.

Round 80: K1, * [yon twice, sl1, K2tog, psso] twice, yfwd, K2tog, yfwd, K5, yfwd, sl1, K1, psso, yfwd, sl1, K2tog, psso, [yon twice, sl1, K2tog, psso] twice, rep from *

to end.

Round 82: K1, * yon twice, sl1, K2tog, psso, yon twice, sl1, K1, psso, K2tog, yfwd, K7, yfwd, sl1, K1, psso, K2tog, [yon twice, sl1, K2tog, psso] twice, rep from * to end.

Round 84: K1, * yon twice, sl1, K2tog, psso, yon twice, K3tog, yfwd, K9, yfwd, K3tog tbl, [yon twice, sl1, K2tog, psso] twice, rep from * to end.

Round 86: K1, * yon twice, sl1, K2tog, psso, yfwd, K2tog, yfwd, K11, yfwd, sl1, K1, psso, yfwd, sl1, K2tog, psso, yon twice, sl1, K2tog, psso, rep from * to end.

Round 88: K1, * yon twice, sl1, K1, psso, K2tog, yfwd, K13, yfwd, sl1, K1, psso, K2tog, yon twice, sl1, K2tog, psso, rep from * to end.

Round 90: K1, * yon twice, K3tog, yfwd, K15, yfwd, K3tog tbl, yon twice, sl1, K2tog, psso, rep from * to end.

Round 92: K1, * yfwd, K2tog, yfwd, K17, yfwd, sl1, K1, psso, yfwd, sl1, K2tog, psso, rep from * to end.

Round 94: * K2tog, yfwd, K19, yfwd, sl1, K1, psso, K1, rep from * to end.

Round 95: K to last 2 sts, these 2 sts will form first 2 sts of next round.

Replace marker here to indicate new start of rounds.

Round 96: * Sl1, K2tog, psso, yfwd, K21, yfwd, rep from * to end.

Round 98: * K1 tbl, yfwd, K23, yfwd, rep from * to end. *520 sts*

Rounds 100 and 101: Knit.

Round 102: * Inc into next st, K25,

rep from * to end. *540 sts*

Round 104: K1, * yfwd, K9, rep
from * to end. *600 sts*

Round 106: * Yfwd, K1 tbl, yfwd,
sl1, K1, psso, K5, K2tog, rep from
* to end.

Round 108: * Yon twice, sl1, K2tog,
psso, yon twice, sl1, K1, psso, K3,
K2tog, rep from * to end.

Round 110: * Yfwd, K1 tbl, yon
twice, sl1, K2tog, psso, yon twice,
K1 tbl, yfwd, sl1, K1, psso, K1,
K2tog, rep from * to end. *720 sts*

Round 112: * Yon twice, sl1, K2tog,
psso, rep from * to end.

Rounds 114: K1, * yon twice, sl1,
K2tog, psso, rep from * to end.

Round 115: As round 3, working
K1, P1 into each double yon of
previous round.

Rounds 116 to 153: Work 38 reps
of rounds 114 and 115.
Bind off.

FINISHING
Sew up waist seam. Stitch length of
elastic to inside of rib at waist.

Skating Skirt

SIZE

One size

Waist approximately 45⅝in (can be adjusted with ribbon)

Length approximately 17⅝in

YARN

RYC Bamboo Soft in 1¾oz (50g) balls (100% bamboo), approx 112yd (102m)

    9 x Cream 100 (A)

    5 x Hemp 104 (B)

1⅝yd of 0.6in-wide ribbon

NEEDLES

US 5 32in-long circular needle

GAUGE

25 sts and 30 rows to 4in over stockinette stitch using US 5 needles.

ABBREVIATIONS

See page 142.

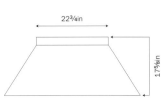

SKIRT

Using US 5 circular needle and yarn A, cast on 120 sts.

Placing round marker and without twisting cast on edge, work as folls:

Round 1: * K1, P1, rep from * to end. Rep this round 5 more times.

Eyelet round 1: * K2tog, yon, rep from * to end.

Work 6 more rounds in K1, P1 rib.

Next round: Knit.

Next round: Purl.

Rep the last 2 rounds once more.

Purl one round.

Now work increase rounds as folls:

Round 1: * K2, yon, rep from * to end. *180 sts*

Knit 4 rounds.

Round 6: * K3, yon, rep from * to end. *240 sts*

Knit 5 rounds.

Round 12: * K4, yon, rep from * to end. *300 sts*

Knit 5 rounds.

Round 18: * K5, yon, rep from * to end. *360 sts*

Knit 5 rounds.

Round 24: * K6, yon, rep from * to end. *420 sts*

Knit 5 rounds.

Round 30: * K7, yon, rep from * to end. *480 sts*

Knit 5 rounds.

Round 36: * K8, yon, rep from * to end. *540 sts*

Purl one round.

Knit 2 rounds.

Round 40: * K9, yon, rep from * to end. *600 sts*

Knit 5 rounds.

Round 46: * K10, yon, rep from * to end. *660 sts*

Knit 3 rounds.

Round 50: * K11, yon, rep from * to end. *720 sts*

Knit 3 rounds.

Round 54: * K12, yon, rep from * to end. *780 sts*

Change to yarn B.

Knit 3 rounds.

Purl 1 round.

Knit 1 round.

Purl 1 round.

Knit 2 rounds.

Purl 1 round.

Change to yarn A.

Eyelet round 2: * K2tog, yon, rep from * to end.

Purl 1 round.

Knit 1 round.

Purl 1 round.

Change to yarn B.

Knit 2 rounds.

Purl 4 rounds.

Knit 3 rounds.

Change to yarn A.

Eyelet round 3: * K2tog, yon, rep from * to end.

Knit 1 round.

Eyelet round 4: Sl1, * yon, K2tog, rep from * to last st, yon, K last st tog with slipped st at start of round.

Purl 1 round.

Knit 1 round.

Rep the last 2 rounds 2 more times.

Bind off.

Thread the ribbon through eyelets in eyelet round 1 at waist.

Puffball Skirt

SIZE

One size

Waist approximately 45⅝in (can be adjusted with ribbon)

Length approximately 22in

YARN

RYC Bamboo Soft in 1¾oz (50g) balls (100% bamboo), approx 82yd (75m)

   17 x Cambria 109

4⅞yd of 0.6in-wide ribbon

NEEDLES

US 5 32in-long circular needle

GAUGE

25 sts and 30 rows to 4in over stockinette stitch using US 5 needles.

ABBREVIATIONS

See page 142.

SKIRT

Using US 5 circular needle, cast on 120 sts.

Placing round marker and without twisting cast on edge, work as for Skating Skirt (see page 90), up to and including eyelet round 4. Then work as folls:

Purl 1 round.

Knit 1 round.

Rep the last 2 rounds 2 more times.

Purl 6 rounds.

Next round: * Insert needle knitwise into 1st st, yon 3 times then knit st, rep from * to end.

Next round: [Purl 1st loop of the triple yon and drop the other 2 loops] into every st.

Purl 7 rounds.

Knit 1 round.

Purl 1 round.

Rep the last 2 rounds 2 more times.

Eyelet round 5: * K2tog, yon, rep from * to end.

Knit 1 round.

Purl 4 rounds.

Knit 1 round.

Purl 1 round.

Bind off purlwise.

Cut ribbons into one 3⅛yd length and one 1⅝yd length. Thread the shorter length of ribbon through eyelets in eyelet round 1 at waist and the longer length through eyelets in eyelet round 5 at hem.

22¾in

22in

Tube dress

SIZE

Small:medium

Bust 31¼:35¼in (when stretched)

16⅞:19¼in (unstretched)

Length 27⅝:28⅞in

YARN

Rowan 4 Ply Soft in 1¾oz (50g) balls (100% merino wool), approx 192yd (175m)

7(8) x Sooty 372 (A)

5(6) x Honk 374 (B)

NEEDLES

Pair of US 3 needles

US 3 32in-long circular needle

US 6 32in-long circular needle

GAUGE

19 sts and 38 rows to 4in over garter stitch using US 6 needles and double yarn.

ABBREVIATIONS

See page 142.

DRESS

Worked down from the top of the garment.

Using US 3 needles and A, cast on 140(160) sts.

Work 4in in K1, P1 rib.

Change to US 3 circular needle and, placing marker and working in rounds, cont rib as set until work measures 19¼(20¼)in from cast on edge.

Shape skirt

Change to US 6 circular needle and use one end each of yarns A and B together.

Work in mock garter stitch (1 round knit, 1 round purl).

Inc round: Knit into front and back of every 10th st. *154(176) sts*

Cont straight for 7 rounds.

Inc round: Knit into front and back of every 11th st. *168(192) sts*

Cont straight for 7 rounds.

Inc round: Knit into front and back of every 12th st. *182(208) sts*

Cont straight for 7 rounds.

Inc round: Knit into front and back of every 13th st. *196(224) sts*

Cont straight for 7 rounds.

Inc round: Knit into front and back of every 14th st. *210(240) sts*

Cont straight for 7 rounds.

Inc round: Knit into front and back of every 15th st. *224(256) sts*

Cont straight until skirt measures 8⅜in.

Bind off loosely.

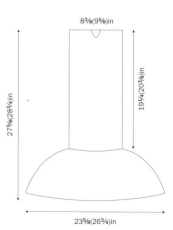

8⅜(9⅝)in

19¼(20⅜)in

27⅝(28¾)in

23⅝(26¾)in

Seersucker Tank Top

SIZE

Small:medium

Bust 43⅝:45⅝in

Length 20⅝:21⅜in

YARN

Rowan Cotton Glace in
1¾oz (50g) balls (100% cotton),
approx 137yd (115m)

  4 x Oyster 730 (A)

  1 x White 9 (B)

NEEDLES

Pair of US 2 needles

US 2 40in-long circular needle

TENSION

32 stitches and 44 rows to 4in over
stockinette stitch using US 2
needles.

ABBREVIATIONS

See page 142.

SPECIAL NOTE

Seersucker stitch

Worked over an even number of sts

Rows 1–7: * K1, P1, rep from *
to end.

Row 8 (WS): P into front and back
of every st.

Rows 9–16: Work in st st.

Row 17: [K2tog] to end.

Rows 18–24: * K1, P1, rep from *
to end.

FRONT PANEL

Using US 2 needles and yarn A,
cast on 50(58) sts.

Rows 1 and 3 (WS): Purl.

Row 2: K1, * sl1 purlwise, K1, rep
from * to last st, K1.

Row 4: K1 * K1, sl1 purlwise, rep
from * to last st, K1.

These 4 rows form the woven st
patt and are repeated.

Work in patt and inc 1 st at each
end of every 6th row until there are
74(82) sts, then work straight until
panel measures 10(10⅞)in, ending
with a WS row.

Leave sts on a spare needle.

BACK AND SIDE PANELS

Using US 2 needles cast on
100 sts.

Work in seersucker st and shape
as folls:

Rows 1–6: * K1, P1, rep from * to
end.

Row 7 (RS): [K1, P1] 5 times,
[K into front and P into back of next
st] twice, * K1, P1, rep from * to
last 12 sts, [K into front and P into
back of next st] twice, [K1, P1]
5 times. *104 sts*

Row 8: P into front and back of
every st.

Rows 9–16: Work in st st.

Row 17: [K2tog] to end.

Row 18: * K1, P1, rep from *
to end.

Row 19: (RS) [K1, P1] 5 times,
[K into front and P into back of next
st] twice, * K1, P1, rep from * to

last 12 sts, [K into front and P into
back of next st] twice, [K1, P1] 5
times. *108 sts*

Rows 20–24: * K1, P1, rep from *
to end.

Rep these 24 rows, twice more.
124 sts

Cont in seersucker st until work
measures same as Front Panel,
ending with a WS row.

Sew to front panel.

With RS facing, slip last 12 sts from
back and side panel onto US 2
circular needle, then 74(82) sts of
front panel, then rem 112 sts of
back and side panel. *198(206) sts*

Place a marker between first
and last st to indicate start of
rounds, first 99(103) sts form the
front and rem 99(103) sts form
the back.

Round 1: K4(0), inc, * K2, inc, rep
from * 29(33) times more, K8(0),
inc, ** K2, inc, rep from ** 29(33)
times more, K4(0). *260(276) sts*

Work in st st (K every round)
without shaping for 2in.

Divide for front and back

Next round: K130(138) sts and
leave these sts on circular needle
for front, then with US 2 needles,
K rem 130(138) sts for back.

BACK

Armhole shaping

Row 1 (WS): [P2tog] 4 times, P to
last 8 sts, [P2tog] 4 times.

Row 2: [K2tog] twice, K to last
4 sts, [K2tog] twice.

Row 3: [P2tog] twice, P to last
4 sts, [P2tog] twice.
Now k2tog (even rows) and p2tog
(odd rows) once at each end of next
5 rows. *104(112) sts*
Work 11 rows in st st.

Back neck shaping

Next row (RS): K20, cast off next
64(72) sts, K to end.
Work in st st on 2nd set of 20 sts
for left strap, leave 1st set of
20 sts on a holder for right strap.
Slipping first st and knitting last st
of every row, dec 1 st at neck edge
on next 8 rows. *12 sts*
Work straight until strap
measures 8⅝in from start
of armhole shaping.
Bind off.
With WS facing, rejoin yarn to
20 sts of right strap and work as
left strap, reversing shaping.

FRONT

Armhole shaping

Row 1: With WS facing, rejoin yarn
to 130(138) sts on circular needle,
[P2tog] 4 times, P to last 8 sts,
[P2tog] 4 times.
Row 2: [K2tog] twice, K to last
4 sts, [K2tog] twice.
Row 3: [P2tog] twice, P to last
4 sts, [P2tog] twice.
Now work 2tog once at each end of
next 5 rows. *104(112) sts*
Work 7 rows in st st.

Front neck shaping

Next row (RS): K20, cast off next
64(72) sts, K to end.

Work in st st on 2nd set of 20 sts
for right strap, leave 1st set of
20 sts on a holder for left strap.
Slipping first st and knitting last st
of every row, dec 1 st at neck edge
on next 8 rows. *12 sts*
Work straight until strap
measures 8⅝in from start
of armhole shaping.
With WS facing, rejoin yarn to 20 sts
of left strap and work as right strap,
reversing shaping.

FINISHING

Join cast off edges of straps.

EDGINGS

Work blanket stitch around neck
and armhole edges using yarn B.

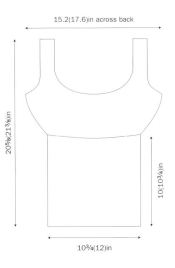

15.2(17.6)in across back

20⅝(21³⁄₈)in

10(10¾)in

10¾(12)in

Peacock Dress

SIZE
Small:medium
Bust 43.6⅝:45⅝in
Length approximately 44⅜:45¼in

YARN
Twilleys Goldfingering in 1¾oz
(50g) balls (80% viscose/
20% polyester), appox 200 yd
(200m)
    13(14) x Burgundy 58

NEEDLES
Pair of US 2 needles
US 2 40in-long and 24in-long
circular needles
US 3 circular needle

GAUGE
32 stitches and 44 rows to
4in over stockinette stitch using US
2 needles.

ABBREVIATIONS
See page 142.

SPECIAL NOTE
Seersucker stitch
Worked over an even number of sts
Rows 1–7: * K1, P1, rep from *
to end.
Row 8 (WS): P into front and back
of every st.
Rows 9–16: Work in st st.
Row 17: [K2tog] to end.
Rows 18–24: * K1, P1, rep from *
to end.

BODICE
FRONT PANEL
Using US 2 needles, cast on
50(58) sts, and work as folls:
Rows 1 and 3 (WS): Purl.
Row 2: K1, * sl1 purlwise, K1, rep
from * to last st, K1.
Row 4: K1 * K1, sl1 purlwise, rep
from * to last st, K1.
These 4 rows form the woven st
patt and are repeated.
Work in patt and inc 1 st each end
of every 6th row until there are
74(82) sts, then work straight until
panel measures 10(10⅞)in, ending
with a WS row.
Leave sts on a spare needle.

BACK AND SIDE PANELS
Using US 2 needles cast on
100 sts.
Work in seersucker st and shape
as folls:
Rows 1–6: * K1, P1, rep from *
to end.
Row 7 (RS): [K1, P1] 5 times, [K
into front and P into back of next st]
twice, * K1, P1, rep from * to last
12 sts, [K into front and P into back
of next st] twice, [K1, P1] 5 times.
104 sts
Row 8: P into front and back of
every st.
Rows 9–16: Work in st st.
Row 17: [K2tog] to end.
Row 18: * K1, P1, rep from *
to end.
Row 19: (RS) [K1, P1] 5 times,
[K into front and P into back of next
st] twice, * K1, P1, rep from * to
last 12 sts, [K into front and P into
back of next st] twice, [K1, P1] 5
times. *108 sts*
Rows 20–24: * K1, P1, rep from *
to end.
Rep these 24 rows, twice more.
124 sts
Cont in seersucker st until work
measures same as Front Panel,
ending with a WS row.
Sew to front panel.
With RS facing, slip last 12 sts from
back and side panel onto US 2
circular needle, then 74(82) sts of
front panel, then rem 112 sts of
back and side panel. *198(206) sts*
Place a marker between first and
last st to indicate start of rounds,
first 99(103) sts form the front and
rem 99(103) sts form the back.
Round 1: [Inc] 99(103) times,
(these 198(206) sts form the front),
K4(0), inc, * K2, inc, rep from *
29(33) times more, K4(0) (the last
130(138) sts form the back).
328(344) sts
Work in st st (K every round)
without shaping for 2in.
Divide for front and back
Next round: K198(206) sts and
leave these sts on circular needle
for front, then with US 2 needles,
K rem 130(138) sts for back.

BACK
Armhole shaping
Row 1 (WS): [P2tog] 4 times, P to
last 8 sts, [P2tog] 4 times.

Row 2: [K2tog] twice, K to last
4 sts, [K2tog] twice.

Row 3: [P2tog] twice, P to last
4 sts, [P2tog] twice.

Now k2tog (even rows) and p2tog
(odd rows) once at each end of next
5 rows. *104(112) sts*

Work 11 rows in st st.

Back neck shaping

Next row (RS): K20, cast off next
64(72) sts, K to end.

Work in st st on 2nd set of 20 sts
for left strap, leave 1st set of
20 sts on a holder for right strap.

Slipping first st and knitting last st
of every row, dec 1 st at neck edge
on next 8 rows. *12 sts*

Work straight until strap
measures 8⅝in from start
of armhole shaping.

Bind off.

With WS facing, rejoin yarn to
20 sts of right strap and work as
left strap, reversing shaping.

FRONT

Armhole shaping

Row 1: With WS facing, rejoin yarn
to 198(206) sts on circular needle,
[P2tog] 4 times, P to last 8 sts,
[P2tog] 4 times.

Row 2: [K2tog] twice, K to last
4 sts, [K2tog] twice.

Row 3: [P2tog] twice, P to last
4 sts, [P2tog] twice.

Work 2tog at each end of next
5 rows. *172(180) sts*

Work 7 rows in st st.

Front neck shaping

Next row (RS): K20, cast off next
132(140) sts, K to end.

Work in st st on 2nd set of 20 sts
for right strap, leave 1st set of

20 sts on a holder for left strap.

Slipping first st and knitting last st
of every row, dec 1 st at neck edge
on next 8 rows. *12 sts*

Work straight until strap
measures 8⅝in from start
of armhole shaping.

With WS facing, rejoin yarn to
20 sts of left strap and work as
right strap, reversing shaping.

NECK EDGING

Join cast off edges of straps.

With US 2 long circular needle, pick
up and knit 342(358) sts evenly
around neck edge.

Round 1: Knit.

Bind off.

ARMHOLE EDGING

With US 2 short circular needle,
pick up and knit 138 sts evenly
around armhole edge.

Work as neck edging.

SKIRT

With RS facing and US 3 circular
needle, pick up and knit 140(160)
sts around lower edge of bodice.
(If preferred, sts can be cast on and
the skirt knitted separately then
sewn to the lower edge of the
bodice on completion.)

Place a round marker.

Rib round: * K1, P1, rep from *
to end.

This round forms rib and is
repeated.

Work in rib for 2⅞in.

1st size only

Round 1: Knit.

Round 2: * Yfwd, K1 tbl, yfwd, K13,
rep from * to end. *160 sts*

Both sizes

Round 3: [K1 tbl] in every st.

Round 4: * Yon twice, sl1, K2tog,
psso, yon twice, sl1, K1, psso, K9,
K2tog, rep from * to end.

Round 5 and every foll alt round: As
round 3, working K1, P1 into each
double yon of previous round.

Round 6: * Yfwd, K1 tbl, yon twice,
sl1, K2tog, psso, yon twice, K1tbl,
yfwd, sl1, K1, psso, K7, K2tog, rep
from * to end. *180 sts*

Round 8: * [Yon twice, sl1, K2tog,
psso] 3 times, yon twice, sl1, K1,
psso, K5, K2tog, rep from * to end.

Round 10: * Yfwd, K1 tbl, [yon
twice, sl1, K2tog, psso] 3 times, yon
twice, K1 tbl, yfwd, sl1, K1, psso,
K3, K2tog, rep from * to end. *200 sts*

Round 12: * [Yon twice, sl1, K2tog,
psso] 5 times, yon twice, sl1, K1,
psso, K1, K2tog, rep from * to end.

Round 14: * Yfwd, K1 tbl, [yon
twice, sl, K2tog, psso] 5 times, yon
twice, K1 tbl, yfwd, sl1, K2tog,
psso, rep from * to end. *220 sts*

Rounds 16, 18 and 20: * Yfwd, sl1,
K2tog, psso, [yon twice, sl1, K2tog,
psso] 6 times, ywfd, K1 tbl, rep
from * to end.

Round 21: As round 5 to last 2 sts,
these 2 sts will form first 2 sts of
next round.

Replace marker here to indicate
new start of rounds.

Round 22: * Yfwd, K3, yfwd, sl1, K1,
psso, yfwd, sl1, K2tog, psso, [yon
twice, sl1, K2tog, psso] 4 times,
yfwd, K2tog, rep from * to end.

Round 24: * Yfwd, K5, yfwd, sl1,
K1, psso, K2tog, [yon twice, sl1,
K2tog, psso] 3 times, yon twice, sl1,
K1, psso, K2tog, rep from * to end.

Round 26: * Yfwd, K7, yfwd, K3tog tbl, [yon twice, sl1, K2tog, psso] 3 times, yon twice, K3tog, rep from * to end.

Round 28: * Yfwd, K9, yfwd, sl1, K1, psso, yfwd, [sl1, K2tog, psso, yon twice] twice, sl1, K2tog, psso, yfwd, K2tog, rep from * to end.

Round 30: * Yfwd, K11, yfwd, sl1, K1, psso, K2tog, yon twice, sl1, K2tog, psso, yon twice, sl1, K1, psso, K2tog, rep from * to end.

Round 32: * Yfwd, K13, yfwd, K3tog tbl, yon twice, sl1, K2tog, psso, yon twice, K3tog, rep from * to end.

Round 34: * Yfwd, K15, yfwd, sl1, K1, psso, yfwd, sl1, K2tog, psso, yfwd, K2tog, rep from * to end.

Round 36: * Yfwd, K17, yfwd, sl1, K1, psso, K1, K2tog, rep from * to end.

Round 38: * Yfwd, K19, yfwd, sl1, K2tog, psso, rep from * to end.

Round 40: * Yfwd, K21, yfwd, K1 tbl, rep from * to end. *240 sts*

Round 42: K11, replace marker here for new start of rounds, * yfwd, K1 tbl, yfwd, sl1, K1, psso, K19, K2tog, rep from * to end.

Round 44: * Yon twice, sl1, K2tog, psso, yon twice, sl1, K1, psso, K17, K2tog, rep from * to end.

Round 46: * Yfwd, K1 tbl, yon twice, sl1, K2tog, psso, yon twice, K1 tbl, yfwd, sl1, K1, psso, K15, K2tog, rep from * to end. *260 sts*

Round 48: * [Yon twice, sl1, K2tog, psso] 3 times, yon twice, sl1, K1, psso, K13, K2tog, rep from * to end.

Round 50: * Yfwd, K1 tbl, [yon twice, sl1, K2tog, psso] 3 times, yon twice, K1 tbl, yfwd, sl1, K1, psso, K11, K2tog, rep from * to end. *280 sts*

Round 52: * [Yon twice, sl1, K2tog, psso] 5 times, yon twice, sl1, K1, psso, K9, K2tog, rep from * to end.

Round 54: * Yon twice, K1 tbl, [yon twice, sl1, K2tog, psso] 5 times, yon twice, K1 tbl, yon twice, sl1, K1, psso, K7, K2tog, rep from * to end. *320 sts*

Round 56: * Yon twice, K1 tbl, [yon twice, sl1, K2tog, psso] 7 times, yon twice, K1 tbl, yon twice, sl1, K1, psso, K5, K2tog, rep from * to end. *360 sts*

Round 58: * Yon twice, K1 tbl, [yon twice, sl1, K2tog, psso] 9 times, yon twice, K1 tbl, yon twice, sl1, K1, psso, K3, K2tog, rep from * to end. *400 sts*

Round 60: * Yon twice, K1 tbl, [yon twice, sl1, K2tog, psso] 11 times, yon twice, K1 tbl, yon twice, sl1, K1, psso, K1, K2tog, rep from * to end. *440 sts*

Round 62: * Yon twice, K1 tbl, [yon twice, sl1, K2tog, psso] 13 times, yon twice, K1 tbl, yon twice, sl1, K2tog, psso , rep from * to end. *480 sts*

Rounds 64, 66, 68 and 70: K1, * yon twice, sl1, K2tog, psso, rep from * to end.

Round 72: K1, * [yon twice, sl1, K2tog, psso] 3 times, yfwd, K1, inc into next st, K1, yfwd, sl1, K2tog, psso, [yon twice, sl1, K2tog, psso] 3 times, rep from * to end. *500 sts*

Round 74: K1, * [yon twice, sl1, K2tog, psso] 3 times, yfwd, K2tog, yfwd, sl1, K1, psso, yfwd, sl1, K2tog, psso, [yon twice, sl1, K2tog, psso] 3 times, rep from * to end. *480 sts*

Round 76: K1, * [Yon twice, sl1,

K2tog, psso] twice, yon twice, sl1, K1, psso, K2tog, yfwd, K1 tbl, yfwd, sl1, K1, psso, K2tog, [yon twice, sl1, K2tog, psso] 3 times, rep from * to end.

Round 78: K1, * [yon twice, sl1, K2tog, psso] twice, yon twice, K3tog, yfwd, K3, yfwd, K3tog tbl, [yon twice, sl1, K2tog, psso] 3 times, rep from * to end.

Round 80: K1, * [yon twice, sl1, K2tog, psso] twice, yfwd, K2tog, yfwd, K5, yfwd, sl1, K1, psso, yfwd, sl1, K2tog, psso, [yon twice, sl1, K2tog, psso] twice, rep from * to end.

Round 82: K1, * yon twice, sl1, K2tog, psso, yon twice, sl1, K1, psso, K2tog, yfwd, K7, yfwd, sl1, K1, psso, K2tog, [yon twice, sl1, K2tog, psso] twice, rep from * to end.

Round 84: K1, * yon twice, sl1, K2tog, psso, yon twice, K3tog, yfwd, K9, yfwd, K3tog tbl, [yon twice, sl1, K2tog, psso] twice, rep from * to end.

Round 86: K1, * yon twice, sl1, K2tog, psso, yfwd, K2tog, yfwd, K11, yfwd, sl1, K1, psso, yfwd, sl1, K2tog, psso, yon twice, sl1, K2tog, psso, rep from * to end.

Round 88: K1, * yon twice, sl1, K1, psso, K2tog, yfwd, K13, yfwd, sl1, K1, psso, K2tog, yon twice, sl1, K2tog, psso, rep from * to end.

Round 90: K1, * yon twice, K3tog, yfwd, K15, yfwd, K3tog tbl, yon twice, sl1, K2tog, psso, rep from * to end.

Round 92: K1, * yfwd, K2tog, yfwd, K17, yfwd, sl1, K1, psso, yfwd, sl1, K2tog, psso, rep from * to end.

Round 94: * K2tog, yfwd, K19, yfwd, sl1, K1, psso, K1, rep from * to end.

Round 95: K to last 2 sts, these 2 sts form first 2 sts of next round. Replace marker here to indicate new start of rounds.

Round 96: * Sl1, K2tog, psso, yfwd, K21, yfwd, rep from * to end.

Round 98: * K1 tbl, yfwd, K23, yfwd, rep from * to end. *520 sts*

Round 100 and 101: Knit.

Round 102: * Inc into next st, K25, rep from * to end. *540 sts*

Round 104: K1, * yfwd, K9, rep from * to end. *600 sts*

Round 106: * Yfwd, K1 tbl, yfwd, sl1, K1, psso, K5, K2tog, rep from * to end.

Round 108: * Yon twice, sl1, K2tog, psso, yon twice, sl1, K1, psso, K3, K2tog, rep from * to end.

Round 110: * Yfwd, K1 tbl, yon twice, sl1, K2tog, psso, yon twice, K1 tbl, yfwd, sl1, K1, psso, K1, K2tog, rep from * to end. *720 sts*

Round 112: * Yon twice, sl1, K2tog, psso, rep from * to end.

Rounds 114: K1, * yon twice, sl1, K2tog, psso, rep from * to end.
Round 115: As round 3, working K1, P1 into each double yon of previous round.

Rounds 116 to 163: Work 48 reps of rounds 114 and 115.

Round 164: As round 114.

Round 165: * [K1, p1, K1] into each 'yon twice', K1, rep from * to end. *960 sts*

Rounds 166 and 167: Knit.

Round 168: * K19, inc into next st, K4, rep from * to end. *1000 sts*

Round 169: K to last 5 sts, these 5 sts will form first 5 sts of next round. Replace marker here to indicate new start of rounds.

Round 170: * Yon 3 times, sl1, K1, psso, yfwd, K21, yfwd, K2tog, rep from * to end. *1120 sts*

Round 171: * [K1, p1] 5 times into each 'yon 3 times', K25, rep from * to end. *1400 sts*

Round 172: * K10, sl1, K1, psso, yfwd, sl1, K1, psso, K17, K2tog, yfwd, K2tog, rep from * to end. *1320 sts*

Round 174: * K10, sl1, K1, psso, yfwd, sl1, K1, psso, K15, K2tog, yfwd, K2tog, rep from * to end. *1240 sts*

Round 176: * Yfwd, K2tog, [yon twice, sl1, K2tog, psso] twice, yon twice, [sl1, K1, psso, yfwd] twice, sl1, K1, psso, K13, K2tog, yfwd, k2tog, rep from * to end.

Round 178: * Yfwd, [sl1, K2tog, psso, yon twice] 3 times, sl1, K2tog, psso, [yfwd, sl1, K1, psso] twice, K11, K2tog, yfwd, K2tog, rep from * to end. *1160 sts*

Round 180: * Yfwd, [sl1, K2tog, psso, yon twice] 3 times, sl1, K2tog, psso, [yfwd, sl1, K1, psso] twice, K9, K2tog, yfwd, K2tog, rep from * to end. *1080 sts*

Round 182: * Yfwd, [sl1, K2tog, psso, yon twice] 3 times, sl1, K2tog, psso, [yfwd, sl1, K1, psso] twice, K7, K2tog, yfwd, K2tog, rep from * to end. *1000 sts*

Round 184: Yfwd, [sl1, K2tog, psso, yon twice] 3 times, sl1, K2tog, psso, [yfwd, sl1, K1, psso] twice, K5, K2tog, yfwd, K2tog, rep from * to end. *920 sts*

Round 186: * Yfwd, [sl1, K2tog, psso, yon twice] 3 times, sl1, K2tog, psso, [yfwd, sl1, K1, psso] twice, K3, K2tog, yfwd, K2tog, rep from * to end. *840 sts*

Round 188: * Yfwd, [sl1, K2tog, psso, yon twice] 3 times, sl1, K2tog, psso, [yfwd, sl1, K1, psso] twice, K1, K2tog, yfwd, K2tog, rep from * to end. *760 sts*

Bind off.

15¼in

20⅝(21⅜)in

44⅜(45¼)in

42¾in

Lurex Tank Top

SIZE
Small:medium
Bust 43⅝:45⅝in
Length 20⅝:21.4⅜in

YARN
Twilleys Goldfingering in 1¾oz (50g) balls (80% viscose/20% polyester), appox 200yd (200m)

4(4) x Navy 55

Shirring elastic

NEEDLES
Pair of US 2 needles
US 2 40in-long and 24in-long circular needles

TENSION
32 stitches and 44 rows to 4in over stockinette stitch using US 2 needles.

ABBREVIATIONS
See page 142.

SPECIAL NOTE
Seersucker stitch
Worked over an even number of sts
Rows 1–7: * K1, P1, rep from * to end.
Row 8 (WS): P into front and back of every st.
Rows 9–16: Work in st st.
Row 17: [K2tog] to end.
Rows 18–24: * K1, P1, rep from * to end.

FRONT PANEL
Using US 2 needles, cast on 50(58) sts, and work as folls:
Rows 1 and 3 (WS): Purl.
Row 2: K1, * sl1 purlwise, K1, rep from * to last st, K1.
Row 4: K1 * K1, sl1 purlwise, rep from * to last st, K1.
These 4 rows form the woven st patt and are repeated.
Work in patt and inc 1 st each end of every 6th row until there are 74(82) sts, then work straight until panel measures 10(10⅞)in, ending with a WS row.
Leave sts on a spare needle.

BACK AND SIDE PANELS
Using US 2 needles, cast on 100 sts. Work in seersucker st and shape as folls:
Rows 1–6: * K1, P1, rep from * to end.
Row 7 (RS): [K1, P1] 5 times, [K into front and P into back of next st] twice, * K1, P1, rep from * to last 12 sts, [K into front and P into back of next st] twice, [K1, P1] 5 times. *104 sts*
Row 8: P into front and back of every st.
Rows 9–16: Work in st st.
Row 17: [K2tog] to end.
Row 18: * K1, P1, rep from * to end.
Row 19: (RS) [K1, P1] 5 times, [K into front and P into back of next st] twice, * K1, P1, rep from * to last 12 sts, [K into front and P into back of next st] twice, [K1, P1] 5 times. *108 sts*

Rows 20–24: * K1, P1, rep from * to end.
Rep these 24 rows, twice more. *124 sts*
Cont in seersucker st until work measures same as Front Panel, ending with a WS row.
Sew to front panel.
With RS facing, slip last 12 sts from back and side panel onto US 2 circular needle, then 74(82) sts of front panel, then rem 112 sts of back and side panel. *198(206) sts*
Place a marker between first and last st to indicate start of rounds, first 99(103) sts form the front and rem 99(103) sts form the back.
Round 1: [Inc] 99(103) times, (these 198(206) sts form the front), K4(0), inc, * K2, inc, rep from * 29(33) times more, K4(0) (the last 130(138) sts form the back). *328(344) sts*
Work in st st (K every round) without shaping for 2in.
Divide for front and back
Next round: K198(206) sts and leave these sts on circular needle for front, then with US 2 needles, K rem 130(138) sts for back.

BACK
Armhole shaping
Row 1 (WS): [P2tog] 4 times, P to last 8 sts, [P2tog] 4 times.
Row 2: [K2tog] twice, K to last 4 sts, [K2tog] twice.
Row 3: [P2tog] twice, P to last 4 sts, [P2tog] twice.

Now work 2tog once at each end of next 5 rows. *104(112) sts*
Work 11 rows in st st.

Back neck shaping

Next row (RS): K20, cast off next 64(72) sts, K to end.

Work in st st on 2nd set of 20 sts for left strap, leave 1st set of 20 sts on a holder for right strap.

Slipping first st and knitting last st of every row, dec 1 st at neck edge on next 8 rows. *12 sts*

Work straight until strap measures 8⅝in from start of armhole shaping.

Bind off.

With WS facing, rejoin yarn to 20 sts of right strap and work as left strap, reversing shaping.

FRONT

Armhole shaping

Row 1: With WS facing, rejoin yarn to 198(206) sts on circular needle, [P2tog] 4 times, P to last 8 sts, [P2tog] 4 times.

Row 2: [K2tog] twice, K to last 4 sts, [K2tog] twice.

Row 3: [P2tog] twice, P to last 4 sts, [P2tog] twice.

Work 2tog at each end of next 5 rows. *172(180) sts*

Work 7 rows in st st.

Front neck shaping

Next row (RS): K20, cast off next 132(140) sts, K to end.

Work in st st on 2nd set of 20 sts for right strap, leave 1st set of 20 sts on a holder for left strap.

Slipping first st and knitting last st of every row, dec 1 st at neck edge on next 8 rows. *12 sts*

Work straight until strap

measures 8⅝in from start of armhole shaping.

With WS facing, rejoin yarn to 20 sts of left strap and work as right strap, reversing shaping.

FINISHING

Join cast off edges of straps for shoulders.

NECK EDGING

With US 2 long circular needle, pick up and knit 342(358) sts evenly around neck edge.

Round 1: Knit.

Round 2: [K2tog, yfwd] to end.

Round 3: Knit.

Bind off.

Turn edging onto WS and slipstitch in place. Thread shirring elastic through edging.

ARMHOLE EDGING

With US 2 short circular needle, pick up and knit 138 sts evenly around armhole edge.

Work exactly as neck edging.

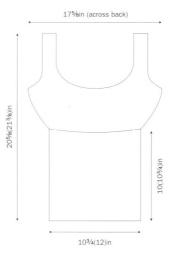

17⅝in (across back)

20⅜(21¾)in

10(10¾)in

10¾(12)in

Chevron Waffle Cardigan

SIZE

Small:medium

Bust 52⅞in

Length 16⅞:17⅝in

Sleeve 18⅞in

YARN

Rowan 4 Ply in 1¾oz (50g) balls
(100% cotton), approx 192yd
(175m)

9(10) x Victoria 390

NEEDLES

Pair of US 3 needles

GAUGE

28 sts and 36 rows to 4in
measured over stockinette stitch
using US 3 needles

ABBREVIATIONS

See page 142.

BACK

Using US 3 needles, cast on
181 sts.

Foundation row: Knit into back of
every stitch.

Row 1 (RS): * P1, M1, P12, P2tog,
P1, P2tog tbl, P12, M1, rep from *
to last st, P1.

Row 2: Knit.

Row 3: * K1, M1, K12, sl1, K1,
psso, k1, K2tog, K12, M1, rep from
* to last st, K1.

Row 4: Purl.

Row 5: * K1, M1, K13, sl 2, K1,
p2sso, K13, M1, rep from * to last
st, K1.

Row 6: Knit.

These 6 rows form the chevron
patt. Work 20 more patt rows, so
ending with patt row 2.

Starting with a K row, work in
st st until back measures
9⅝(10⅜)in, ending with a P row.

Shape armholes

Bind off 2 sts at beg of next
2 rows. *177 sts*

Cont straight until armhole
measures 3⅝in, ending with a P row.

Next row (RS): P1, * K1tbl, P2, rep
from * to last 2 sts, K1tbl, P1.

Next row: K1, P1tbl, * K2, P1tbl, rep
from * to last st, K1.

These 2 rows form waffle patt and
are repeated.

Cont in patt until armhole measures
6⅞in, ending with a WS row.

Shape shoulders and back neck

Next row: Bind off 15 sts, patt until
you have 50 sts on your right-hand

needle, turn and work this side
first, leave rem sts on a holder.

Next row (WS): Bind off 18 sts, patt
to end. *32 sts*

Next row: Bind off 15 sts, patt to
end. *17 sts*

Next row: Dec 1 st, patt to end.
Bind off rem 16 sts.

Rejoin yarn to rem 112 sts on
holder, cast off center 47 sts, patt
to end.

Work to match first side, reversing
all shapings.

LEFT FRONT

Using US 3 needles, cast on
91 sts.

Foundation row: Knit into back of
every st.

Work 26 rows of chevron patt as
set for Back, so ending with patt
row 2.

Starting with a K row, work in st st
until front measures 9⅝(10⅜)in,
ending with a P row.

Shape armholes and front neck

Next row (RS): Bind off 2 sts at beg
of next row, K to last 4 sts, K2tog,
K2. *88 sts*

Next row: P2, P2tog, P to end.

Next row: K to last 5 sts, K3tog, K2.
Rep these 2 rows until 47 sts rem.
Cont straight until armhole
measures 3⅝in, ending with a P
row.

Next row (RS): P2, * K1tbl, P2, rep
from * to end.

Next row: K2, * P1tbl, K2, rep from
* to end.

These 2 rows set waffle patt.

Cont in patt until armhole measures 6¾in, ending with RS facing for next row.

Shape shoulders

Bind off 15 sts at beg of next and foll alt row.

Work 1 row.

Bind off rem 17 sts.

RIGHT FRONT

Work as Left Front, reversing all shapings.

SLEEVES

Using US 3 needles, cast on 61(67) sts.

Foundation row: Knit into back of every st.

Working 3 sts in st st at each end of every row for 2nd size only, work 26 rows in chevron patt as given for Back.

Starting with a K row, work 16 rows in st st.

Cont in st st and inc 1 st at each end of next row and every foll 6th(8th) row until there are 101 sts.

Cont straight until sleeve measures 16⅜in from start of st st, ending with a P row.

Shape sleeve top

Bind off 2 sts at beg of next 2 rows. 97 sts

Dec 1 st at each end of next 3 rows, then 3 foll alt rows, then every 4th row until there are 67 sts, then on every row until 61 sts rem.

Bind off.

FRONT BANDS

Join shoulder seams.

With RS facing and US 3 needles, pick up and knit 55 sts up right front, 63 sts along right front neck, 43 sts from back neck, 63 sts down left front neck, and 55 sts down left front. 279 sts

Row 1: K1, * P1, K1, rep from * to end

This row forms seed st.

Work 4 more rows in seed st.

Bind off.

FRONT TIES

(make 2)

Using US 3 needles, cast on 5 sts.

Work in seed st as given for Front Bands until tie measures 16in.

Bind off.

Attach 1 tie on each front, 8⅜in up from cast on edge.

FINISHING

Join side seams. Join sleeve seams. Insert sleeves into armholes, gathering top section into small pleats.

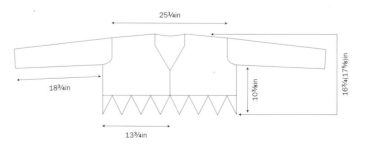

Lace and Chevron Cardigan

SIZE
Small:medium
Bust 43⅝in
Length 22⅜:23¼in
Sleeve 18¾in

YARN
Rowan Cotton Glace Soft in 1¾oz
(50g) balls (100% cotton), approx
137yd (115m)
 11(12) x Ecru 725

NEEDLES
Pair of US 3 needles

GAUGE
23 sts and 32 rows to 4in
measured over stockinette stitch
using US 3 needles.

ABBREVIATIONS
See page 142.

SPECIAL NOTE:
Lace pattern
Row 1 (RS): Knit.
Row 2: Purl.
Row 3: K1, * K2tog twice, [yfwd,
k1] 5 times, [K2tog] 3 times, rep
from * to end.
Row 4: Purl.

BACK
Using US 3 needles, cast on 181
sts.
Foundation row: Knit into back of
every stitch
Row 1 (RS): * P1, M1, P12, P2tog,
P1, P2tog tbl, P12, M1, rep from *
to last st, P1.
Row 2: Knit.
Row 3: * K1, M1, K12, sl1, K1,
psso, k1, K2tog, K12, M1, rep from
* to last st, K1.
Row 4: Purl.
Row 5: * K1, M1, K13, sl2, K1,
p2sso, K13, M1, rep from * to last
st, K1.
Row 6: Knit.
These 6 rows form chevron patt.
Work 20 more patt rows, so ending
with patt row 2.
Starting with a K row, work in lace
stitch until back measures
9⅝(10⅜)in from start of lace
stitch, ending with RS facing for
next row.
Shape armholes
Bind off 15 sts at beg of next
2 rows. *151 sts*
Cont straight until armhole
measures approximately 5¼in,
ending with row 2 of lace patt.
Dec row (RS): K1, * K2tog, K1, rep
from * to end. *101 sts*
Next row: Knit.
Next row: Purl.
Next row: Knit.
Next row: Knit.
Next row: Purl.
Next row: Knit.

The last 6 rows form ridge patt and
are repeated 5 times more, then
the 1st 3 rows again.
Shape shoulders
Bind off 31 sts at beg of next
2 rows. *39 sts*
Leave rem sts on a holder.

LEFT FRONT
Using US 3 needles, cast on
91 sts.
Foundation row: Knit into back of
every st.
Work 26 rows of chevron patt
as set for Back, ending with patt
row 2.
Starting with a K row, work in lace
stitch until front measures
9⅝(10⅜)in from start of lace
stitch, ending with RS facing for
next row.
Shape armholes and front neck
Next row: Bind off 15 sts at beg of
next row, patt to last 2 sts, K2tog.
76 sts
Keeping patt correct, cont in patt
and dec 1 st at front edge on every
following 4th row until 69 sts rem.
Cont straight until armhole
measures approximately 3¾in,
ending with row 2 of lace patt.
Dec row (RS): K1, * K2tog, K1, rep
from * to last st, K1. *48 sts*
Work in ridge patt as given for Back
and dec 1 st at front edge on every
RS row until 31 sts rem.
Cont straight until front matches
Back to shoulder, ending with a
WS row.

Shape shoulder
Bind off.

RIGHT FRONT

Work as Left Front, reversing
all shapings.

SLEEVES

Using US 3 needles, cast on
61 sts.

Foundation row: Knit into back of
every st.

Work 26 rows in chevron patt as
given for Back.

Inc row (RS): K1, * M1, K2, rep
from * to end. *91 sts*

Purl 1 row.

Starting with row 1, work in lace
stitch until sleeve measures
approximately 14⅜in from start of
lace stitch, ending with RS facing
for next row.

Shape sleeve top
Bind off 15 sts at beg of next
2 rows. *61 sts*

Keeping patt correct, dec 1 st at
each end of next row and 4 foll
4th rows. *51 sts*

Cont straight until sleeve top
measures approximately 3¾in,
ending with row 2 of lace patt.

Next row (RS): K2tog, K to last
2 sts, K2tog.

Next row: Knit.

Next row: P2tog, P to last 2 sts,
P2tog.

Next row: Knit.

Next row: K2tog, K to last 2 sts,
K2tog.

Next row: Purl.

These 6 rows form the ridge patt
with decreases and are repeated
4 more times. *21 sts*

Bind off.

SLEEVE EDGINGS

With RS facing and US 3 needles,
pick up and knit 81 sts along cast
on edge of sleeve.

Starting with a P row, work 11 rows
in st st.

Picot row (RS): K1, * yfwd, K2tog,
rep from * to end.

Starting with a P row, work 11 rows
in st st.

Bind off loosely.

FRONT BANDS

Join shoulder seams.

With RS facing and US 3 needles,
pick up and knit 91 sts up right
front, 47 sts along right front neck,
knit across 39 sts from back neck
and dec 3 sts evenly, pick up and
knit 47 sts down left front neck,
and 91 sts down left front. *312 sts*

Row 1: K1, * P1, K1, rep from *
to end.

This row forms seed st and is
repeated 10 more times.

Bind off in seed st.

FRONT TIES

(make 2)

Using US 3 needles, cast on
11 sts.

Work in seed st as given for Front
Bands until tie measures 16in.

Bind off in seed st.

Attach 1 tie on each front, 12⅜in
up from cast on edge.

FINISHING

Fold sleeve edging onto WS along
picot row and slipstitch cast off
edge to pick up row. Join side
seam. Join sleeve seam. Sew
sleeves into armholes, gathering
top section into small pleats to fit.

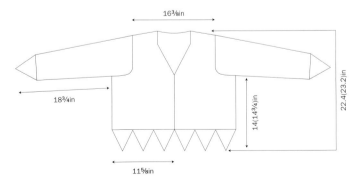

Tweed Cardigan

SIZE

One size

Bust 31¼in

Length 18in

Sleeve 11¼in

YARN

Rowan Felted Tweed in 1¾oz (50g)
balls (wool blend), approx 192yd
(175m)

   8 x Carbon 159

8 buttons

NEEDLES

Pair of US 8 needles

GAUGE

18 sts and 32 rows to 4in over
seed st and 20 sts and 24 rows
over rib, both on US 8 needles with
yarn used doubled.

ABBREVIATIONS

See page 142.

CENTER BACK

Using US 8 needles and yarn
doubled throughout, cast on 34 sts.
Row 1 (RS): K2, * P2, K2, rep from
* to end.
Row 2: P2, * K2, P2, rep from *
to end.
These 2 rows form rib and
are repeated.
Work in rib patt until back
measures 10in, ending with a
WS row.
Shape back
Inc and take into rib, 1 st at each
end of next row and 4 foll alt rows,
then at each end of every row
until there are 58 sts, ending with
a WS row.
Cont straight in rib for a further 5in.
Bind off.

LEFT BACK

Using US 8 needles and yarn
doubled, cast on 22 sts.
Work in patt as set for Center Back
for 10in, ending with a WS row.
Next row: Patt to last 2 sts, patt 2tog.
Patt 1 row.
Rep the last 2 rows 3 more times.
*18 sts ***
**Shape armholes and center
back shaping**
Next row (RS): Bind off 5 sts, patt
to last 2 sts, patt 2tog. *12 sts*
Dec 1 st at beg (Center Back edge)
of next row. *11 sts*
Dec 1 st at each end of next
3 rows. *5 sts*
Dec 1 st at Center Back on next

3 rows. *2 sts*
Bind off.

RIGHT BACK

Work as Left Back, reversing
all shapings.
Join side backs to Center Back
neatly with seam showing on RS.

POCKET LININGS

(make 2)
Using US 8 needles and yarn
double, cast on 14 sts.
Work in patt as set for Center Back
for 2in, ending with a WS row.
Leave sts on a holder.

LEFT FRONT

Using US 8 needles and yarn
double, cast on 34 sts.
Work in patt as set for Center Back
until work measures 7¼in, ending
with a WS row.
Place pocket
Next row (RS): Patt 12 sts, slip next
14 sts onto a holder, patt across
14 sts of one pocket lining, patt
to end.
Cont in patt until work measures
same as Left Back to **, ending
with a WS row.
Shape armholes and front neck
Next row (RS): Bind off 5 sts at
beg of next row, patt to last 2 sts,
patt 2tog.
Next row: Patt to end.
Dec 1 st at armhole edge of next
3 rows and at the same time dec
1 st at neck edge on next row and

every foll 4th row until 15 sts rem. Cont straight until front measures same as Back to cast off edge, ending with a WS row.

Shoulder panel

Row 1: K1, * P1, K1, rep from * to end.

This row forms seed st and is repeated.

Cont in seed st for 1⅝in, ending with a WS row.

Back neck shaping

Inc 1 st at end (neck edge) of next row and same edge of foll 5 rows. *21 sts*

Bind off.

RIGHT FRONT

Work as Left Front, reversing all shapings.

SLEEVES

Using US 8 needles and yarn double, cast on 53 sts.

Moss st row: K1, * P1, K1, rep from * to end.

Rep this row 3 more times and inc 1 st at end of last row. *54 sts*

Row 1 (RS): K2, * P2, K2, rep from * to end.

Row 2: P2, * K2, P2, rep from * to end.

Work in rib patt until sleeve measures 8⅜in from cast on edge, ending with a WS row.

Cont in rib and inc 1 st at each end of next row and every foll alt row until there are 70 sts, taking all inc sts into patt.

Cont straight until sleeve measures 11¼in, ending with a WS row.

Starting with a P row, work 4 rows in rev st st and inc 4 sts evenly

over last row. *74 sts*

Starting with a K row, work 4 rows in st st.

Starting with a P row, work 4 rows in rev st st and inc 2 sts evenly over last row. *76 sts*

Bind off.

POCKET BORDERS

With RS facing and US 8 needles, work across pocket sts on holder.

Row 1: * K1, P1, rep from * to end.

Row 2: * P1, K1, rep from * to end.

These 2 rows form seed st.

Work 3 more rows in seed st.

Bind off in seed st.

HEM EDGING

Join side and shoulder seams.

With RS facing and US 8 needles, pick up and knit along lower edges, 32 sts along left front, 71 sts along back, 32 sts along right front.

135 sts

Row 1: K1, * P1, K1, rep from * to end.

This row forms seed st.

Work 4 more rows in seed st.

Bind off in seed st.

NECK AND FRONT BORDER

With RS facing and US 8 needles, pick up and knit 57 sts up right front edge, 29 sts up right front neck, 9 sts from right shoulder panel, 23 sts from back neck, 9 sts from left shoulder panel, 29 sts down left front neck and 57 sts down left front edge. *213 sts*

Work 5 rows in seed st as given for Hem Edging.

Bind off in seed st.

FINISHING

Join sleeve seams. Sew sleeves into armholes, easing to fit.

Slipstitch pocket lining and pocket borders in position.

Sew buttons in pairs to left and right front edgings. Make four 3⅝in chains from contrast yarn, fold each chain in half and attach around buttons on right front to loop around buttons on left front.

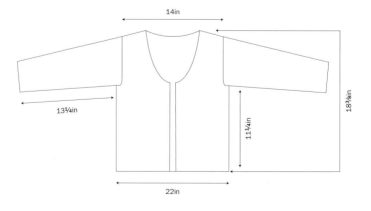

Long Vest

SIZE
One size
Bust 32¾in
Length 30in

YARN
Rowan 4ply Soft in 1¾oz (50g) balls (100% wool), approx 192yd (175m)
    5 x Teak 397 (A)
    6 x Marine 380 (B)
6 buttons

NEEDLES
Pair of US 5 needles

GAUGE
21 sts and 36 rows to 4in over seed st and 20 sts and 30 rows over 2 x 2 rib, both using US 5 needles and double yarn.

ABBREVIATIONS
See page 142.

CENTER BACK
Using US 5 needles and one end each of yarns A and B, cast on 38 sts.
Row 1 (RS): K2, * P2, K2, rep from * to end.
Row 2: P2, * K2, P2, rep from * to end.
These 2 rows form rib and are repeated.
Work in patt until back measures 20⅜in, ending with a WS row.
Shape back
Inc 1 st at each end of next row and 5 foll alt rows then every foll row until there are 62 sts.
Cont straight for 6¾in, ending with a WS row.
Bind off.
Place markers 21 sts in from each end of cast off row.

LEFT BACK
Using US 5 needles and one end each of yarns A and B, cast on 26 sts.
Work patt as set for Center Back for 20⅜in, ending with a WS row.
Next row (RS): Patt to last 2 sts, patt 2tog.
Next row: Patt to end.
Rep the last 2 rows once more.
Shape armholes and Center Back
Next row (RS): Bind off 6 sts, patt to last 2 sts, patt 2tog. *17 sts*
Work 1 row.
Dec 1 st at beg of next row and same edge of foll 4 rows, then 2 foll alt rows and at same time

dec 1 st at end of next and 2 foll alt rows, then at same edge on every row to 2 sts.
Bind off.

RIGHT BACK
Work as Left Back, reversing all shapings.
Join side backs to center back neatly with seam showing on RS.

POCKET LININGS
(make 2)
Using US 5 needles and one end each of yarns A and B, cast on 18 sts.
Work rib patt as set for Center Back until pocket lining measures 2¼in, ending with a WS row, leave sts on a holder.

LEFT FRONT
Using US 5 needles and one end each of yarns A and B, cast on 42 sts.
Work rib patt as set for Center Back until work measures 16⅜in, ending with a WS row.
Place pocket
Next row (RS): Patt 12 sts, slip next 18 sts onto a holder, patt across 18 sts of one pocket lining, patt to end.
Cont in patt until work measures same as Left Back to armhole, ending with a WS row.
Shape armholes and front neck
Next row: Bind off 6 sts, patt to end. *36 sts*

Work 1 row.

Dec 1 st at beg of next row and at same edge of next 3 rows. *32 sts*

Next row (RS): Dec 1 st at beg of next row and 2 foll alt rows and at same time dec 1 st at end of next row and 4 foll alt rows, then every foll 4th row until 15 sts rem.

Cont straight until armhole measures 6⅝in, ending with a WS row.

Shoulder panel

Break off yarn A and join in a 2nd end of yarn B.

Next row: K1, * P1, K1, rep from * to end.

This row forms seed st and is repeated.

Work 5 more rows.

Cont in seed st and inc 1 st at end of next row and at same edge of foll 5 rows. *21 sts*

Bind off.

RIGHT FRONT

Work as Left Front, reversing all shapings.

ARMHOLE BORDERS

(both alike)

Join shoulder seams, using back edge markers as a guide.

With RS facing, US 5 needles and 2 ends of yarn B, pick up and knit 75 sts evenly around armhole edge.

Row 1: K1, * P1, K1, rep from * to end.

This row forms seed st.

Work 5 more rows in seed st.

Bind off in seed st.

POCKET BORDERS

With RS facing, US 5 needles and 2 ends of yarn B, work across 18 pocket sts on holder as folls:

Row 1: * K1, P1, rep from * to end.

Row 2: * P1, K1, rep from * to end.

These 2 rows form seed st.

Work 3 more rows in seed st.

Bind off in seed st.

HEM BORDER

Join side seams.

With RS facing, US 5 needles and using 2 ends of yarn B, pick up along lower edges and knit 38 sts along right front, 81 sts along back and 38 sts along left front. *157 sts*

Work 6 rows in seed st as given for Armhole Borders.

Bind off in seed st.

NECK AND FRONT BORDER

With RS facing, US 5 needles and using 2 ends of yarn B, pick up and knit 84 sts up right front, 26 sts up right front neck, 9 sts along shoulder panel, 21 sts along back neck, 9 sts along left shoulder panel, 26 sts down left front neck, 84 sts down left front. *259 sts*

Work 3 rows in seed st as given for Armhole Borders.

Buttonhole row: Moss st 5, [yon, work 2tog, seed st 13] 5 times, yon, work 2tog, seed st to end.

Work 2 rows in seed st as set.

Bind off in seed st.

FINISHING

Slipstitch pocket linings and borders in place. Sew on buttons.

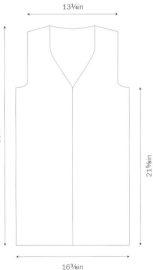

13¼in

30in

21⅝in

16⅜in

Striped Tunic Dress

SIZE

Small:medium
Bust 36:40in
Length 28:28¾in
Sleeve 17¼in

YARN

Rowan 4ply Soft in 1¾oz (50g)
balls (100% merino wool), approx
192yd (175m)

   4(4) x Nippy 376 (A)

Twilleys Goldfingering in 1¾oz (50g)
balls (80% viscose/20% polyester),
appox 200yd (200m)

   6(7) x Copper 52 (B)

NEEDLES

Pair of US 6 needles
Pair of US 7 needles

GAUGE

20 sts and 40 rows to 4in over
garter stitch using US 6 needles.

ABBREVIATIONS

See page 142.

BACK AND FRONT

(both alike)
Using US 6 needles and yarn A,
cast on 92(102) sts.
Work 216 rows in garter st in 4-row
stripes of yarns A and B.

Shape raglans
Row 1 (RS): K3, K2tog, K to last
5 sts, K2tog, K3.
Row 2: K1, P2, K to last 3 sts,
P2, K1.
Rep these 2 rows until 28(30) sts
rem and 16(18) stripes have
been completed from beg of
raglan shaping.
Leave sts on spare needle.

SLEEVES

Using US 6 needles and yarn A,
cast on 39(46) sts.
Work in garter stitch in 4-row
stripes of yarns A and B.
Patt 8 rows.
Next row (RS): K1(2), * inc, K1, rep
from * to end. *58(68) sts*
Change to US 7 needles.

Cont in garter st, and inc 1 st each
end of every following 16th row until
there are 74(84) sts.
Cont straight until work measures
17¼in from cast on edge, ending
with a WS row.

Shape raglans
Row 1 (RS): K3, K2tog, K to last
5 sts, K2tog, K3.
Row 2: K1, P2, K to last 3 sts,
P2, K1.
Rep these two rows until
10(12) sts rem.
Leave sts on a spare needle.

NECKBAND

With RS facing, US 6 needles and
yarn A, cast on 8 sts, knit across
28(30) sts of back, cast on 8 sts,
knit across 10(12) sts of left
sleeve, cast on 8 sts, knit across
28(30) sts of front, cast on 8 sts,
knit across 10(12) sts of right
sleeve. *108(116) sts*
Work 8 rows in garter st.
Bind off knitwise.

FINISHING

Join raglan seams, leaving 5 stripes
at top of all pieces open. Join
neckband seam. Join side and
sleeve seams. Press seams lightly.

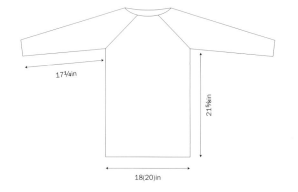

17¼in

21⅝in

18(20)in

Lurex Tunic

SIZE
Small:medium
Bust 31¼:32⅜in
Length 21⅝:22¾in
Sleeve 17¼in

YARN
Twilleys Goldfingering in 1¾oz (50g) balls (80% viscose/20% polyester), appox 200yd (200m)

7(8) x Copper 52

NEEDLES
1 pair US 3 needles
1 pair US 5 needles

GAUGE
28 sts and 50 rows to 4in over garter stitch using US 3 needles.

ABBREVIATIONS
See page 142.

BACK AND FRONT
(both alike)
Using US 3 needles, cast on 110(114) sts.
Work 164 rows in garter st.
Shape raglans
Row 1 (RS): K3, K2tog, K to last 5 sts, K2tog, K3.
Row 2: K1, P2, K to last 3 sts, P2, K1.
Rep these 2 rows until 46(50) sts rem.
Leave sts on a holder.

SLEEVES
Using US 5 needles, cast on 35(43) sts.
Work 8 rows in garter st.
Inc row: K1(2), * inc in next st, rep from * to last 1(2) sts, K1(2). *68(82) sts*
Change to US 3 needles.
Cont in garter st and inc 1 st at each end of 11(8) following 12th(18th) rows. *90(98) sts*

Cont straight until work measures 17¼in from beg.
Shape raglans
Row 1 (RS): K3, K2tog, K to last 5 sts, K2tog, K3.
Row 2: K1, P2, K to last 3 sts, P2, K1.
Rep these 2 rows until 26(34) sts rem.
Leave sts on a holder.

NECKBAND
Using US 3 needles, knit across the 46(50) sts of back, 26(34) sts of the left sleeve, 46(50) sts of front and 26(34) sts of right sleeve. *144(168) sts*
Work 6 rows in garter st.
Bind off knitwise.

FINISHING
Join raglan seams. Join neckband seam. Join side and sleeve seams.

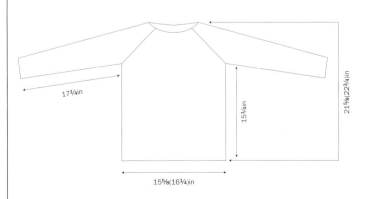

17¼in · 15¼in · 21⅝(22¾)in · 15⅝(16¼)in

Stockinette Stitch Sweater

SIZE

Extra small:small:medium:large

Bust 44¾:46⅜:48¾:50⅜in

Length 26⅜:26¾:27¼:27⅝in

Sleeve 20:20:20⅜:20⅜in

YARN

RYC Cotton Jeans in 1¾oz (50g) balls (100% cotton), approx 82yd (75m)

    16(17:18:19) x Sailcloth 362 (A)

    2 x Canvas 360 (B)

NEEDLES

Pair of US 6 needles

Pair of US 7 needles

GAUGE

19 sts and 26 rows to 4in over stockinette stitch on US 7 needles.

ABBREVIATIONS

See page 142.

BACK

With US 6 needles and yarn B, cast on 110(114:118:122) sts.

Row 1 (RS): K2, * P2, K2, rep from * to end.

Row 2: P2, * K2, P2, rep from * to end.

These 2 rows form rib.

Work 22 more rows in rib and dec 6 sts evenly across last row. *104(108:112:116) sts*

Change to US 7 needles and yarn A.

Beg with a K row, work in st st until back measures 15⅜(15¾:16¼:16⅝)in, ending with a WS row.

Place markers at each end of last row for armholes. **

Cont straight in st st until work measures 10⅜in from markers, ending with a WS row.

Shape shoulders and back neck

Next row (RS): Bind off 12 sts, K until there are 24(26:28:30) sts on right-hand needle, turn and leave rem sts on a holder.

Work each side of neck separately.

Next row: P2tog, P to end. *23(25:27:29) sts*

Next row: Bind off 12 sts, K to last 2 sts, K2tog. *10(12:14:16) sts*

Next row: P2tog, P to end.

Bind off rem 9(11:13:15) sts.

With RS facing, slip center 32 sts onto a stitch holder, rejoin yarn A to rem sts and K to end.

Complete to match first side, reversing all shapings.

FRONT

Work as given for Back to **.

Cont straight in st st until 10 rows less have been worked than on Back to shoulder shaping.

Shape neck

Next row (RS): K40(42:44:46), turn and leave rem sts on a holder.

Work each side of neck separately.

Next row: P to end.

Dec 1 st at neck edge of next 7 rows. *33(35:37:39) sts*

Work 1 row.

Shape shoulder

Bind off 12 sts at beg of next and foll alt row. *9(11:13:15) sts*

Work 1 row.

Bind off rem 9(11:13:15) sts.

With RS facing, slip center 24 sts onto a holder, rejoin yarn to rem sts, K to end.

Complete to match first side, reversing all shapings.

SLEEVES

Using US 6 needles and yarn B, cast on 42(42:46:46) sts.

Work 24 rows in rib as given for Back and dec 4(2:4:2) sts evenly across last row. *38(40:42:44) sts*

Change to US 7 needles and yarn A.

Beg with a K row, work in st st, inc 1 st at each end of next and foll alt row, then at each end of every foll 4th row until there are 90(92:94:96) sts.

Cont straight in st st until sleeve measures 20(20:20⅜:20⅜)in, ending with a WS row.

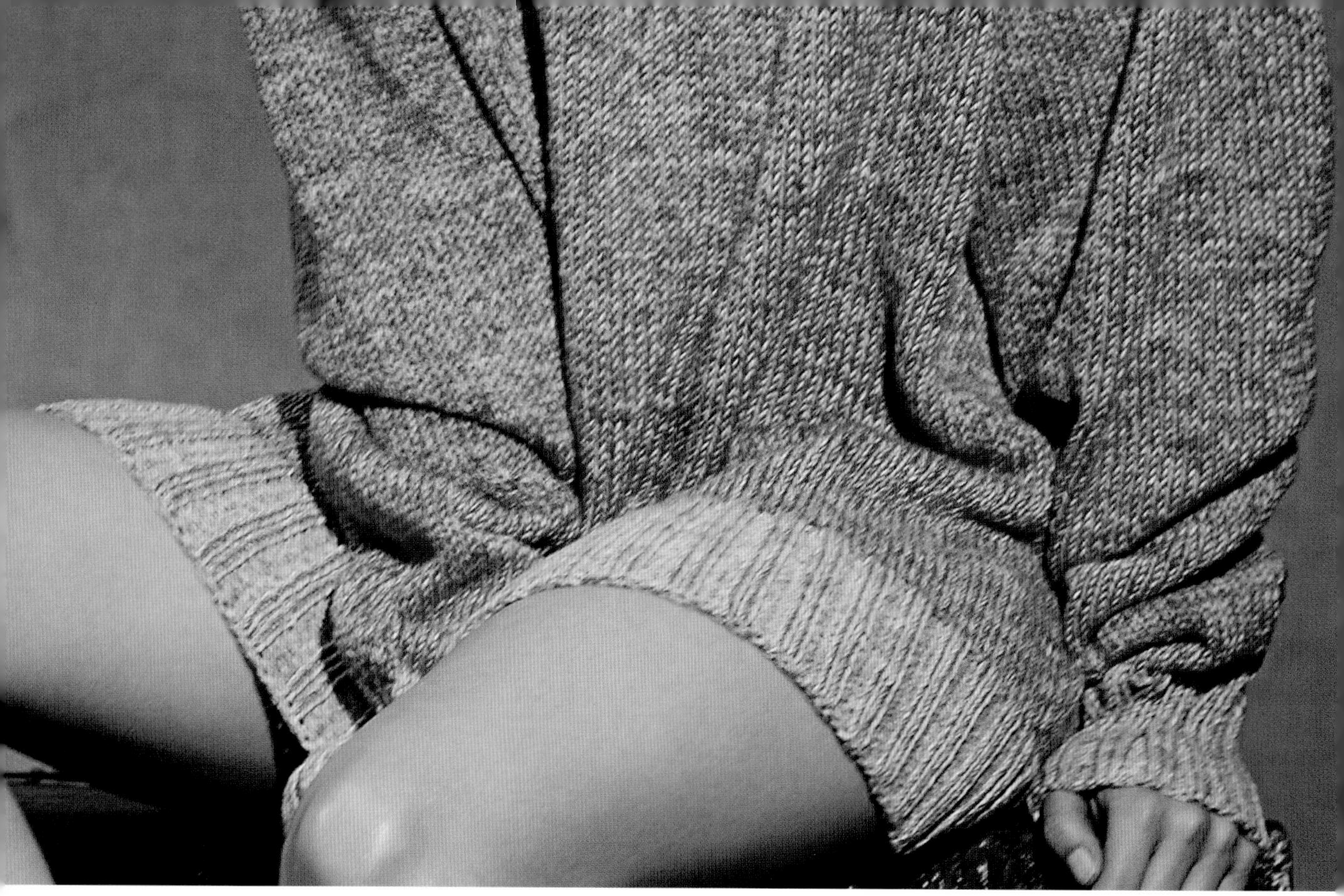

Shape top

Dec 1 st at each end of next row and the 3 foll alt rows then at each end of every row until 42(44:46:48) sts rem.

Bind off 13 sts at beg of next 2 rows.

Bind off rem 16(18:20:22) sts.

COLLAR

Join right shoulder seam.

With RS facing, US 6 needles and yarn B, pick up and knit 13 sts down left front neck, knit across 24 sts on center front holder, pick up and knit 13 sts up right front neck, 4 sts down right back neck, knit across 32 sts on back neck holder, then pick up and knit 4 sts up left back neck. *90 sts*

Beg with row 2 of rib, work until collar measures 4⅜in.

Change to US 7 needles.

Cont in rib until collar measures 8¾in.

Bind off in rib.

FINISHING

Join left shoulder and collar seam, reversing seam on last 4⅜in of collar.

Turn collar onto RS of garment.

Join side seams to markers.

Join sleeve seams.

Sew sleeves into armholes.

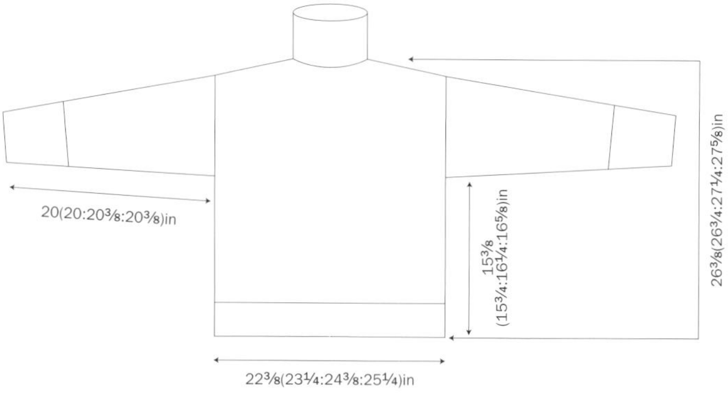

20(20:20⅜:20⅜)in
15⅜ (15¾:16¼:16⅝)in
26⅜(26¾:27¼:27⅝)in
22⅜(23¼:24⅜:25¼)in

Cable and Garter Sweater

SIZE

Extra small:small;medium:large

Bust 44:45⅝:47¼:48in

Length 26⅜:26¾:27¼:27⅝in

Sleeve 21¼:21¼:21⅝:21⅝in

YARN

RYC Cotton Jeans in 1¾oz (50g)
balls (100% cotton), approx 82yd
(75m)

   10(10:11:11) x Jute 361 (A)

Rowan Handknit Cotton in 1¾oz
(50g) balls (cotton), approx 93yd
(85m)

   11(12:12:13) x Linen 205 (B)

NEEDLES

Pair of US 6 needles

Pair of US 7 needles

Cable needle

GAUGE

21 sts and 26 rows to 4in
over cable patt and 20 sts and
35 rows over garter st, both on US
7 needles

ABBREVIATIONS

C6F = slip next 3 sts onto cable
needle and hold at front of work,
k3, then K3 from cable needle.
See also page 142.

BACK

LEFT BACK PANEL

Using US 6 needles and yarn B,
cast on 14(14:18:18) sts.

Row 1 (RS): K2, * P2, K2, rep from
* to end.

Row 2: P2, * K2, P2, rep from *
to end.

These 2 rows form rib.

Work 18 more rows in rib and dec
4(2:4:2) sts evenly across last row.
10(12:14:16) sts

Change to US 7 needles.

Work straight in garter st until panel
measures 15⅜(15¾:16¼:16⅝)in,
ending with a WS row.

Shape armhole

Bind off 5 sts at beg of next row.
5(7:9:11) sts

Work 1 row.

Dec 1 st at beg (armhole edge) of
next 5 rows, then on 0(1:3:5) foll
alt rows.

Fasten off.

RIGHT BACK PANEL

Work as given for Left Back Panel,
reversing shapings and working
1 row more before armhole shaping.

CABLE PANEL

Using US 6 needles and yarn A,
cast on 98 sts.

Work 20 rows in rib as given for
Left Back Panel and dec 4 sts
evenly across last row. *94 sts*

Change to US 7 needles.

Row 1 (RS): K2, * P2, K6, rep from
* to last 4 sts, P2, K2.

Row 2 and every foll alt row: P2, *
K2, P6, rep from * to last 4 sts,
K2, P2.

Row 3: K2, * P2, C6F, P2, K6,
rep from * to last 12 sts, P2, C6F,
P2, K2.

Row 5: As row 1.

Row 6: As row 2.

These 6 rows form cable patt. **
Cont in cable patt until panel
measures 25¾(26¼:26⅝:27)in,
ending with a WS row.

Shape shoulders and back neck

Next row (RS): Keeping patt correct,
cast off 9 sts, patt until there
are 21 sts on right-hand needle,
turn and leave rem sts on a
stitch holder.

Work each side of neck separately.

Next row: Patt 2tog, patt to end.
20 sts

Next row: Bind off 9 sts, patt to last
2 sts, patt 2tog. *10 sts*

Next row: Patt 2tog, patt to end.
Bind off rem 9 sts.

With RS facing, slip center 34 sts
onto a holder, rejoin yarn A to rem
sts and patt to end.

Complete to match first side,
reversing all shapings.

FRONT

Work left and right front panels as
given for Back.

CABLE PANEL

Work as given for cable panel of
Back to **.

Cont straight in cable patt until

12 rows less have been worked than on Back to shoulder shaping.

Shape neck

Next row (RS): Patt 34, turn and leave rem sts on a stitch holder. Work each side of neck separately.

Next row: Patt to end.

Dec 1 st at neck edge of next 5 rows, then on 2 foll alt rows. *27 sts*

Work 1 row.

Shape shoulder

Keeping patt correct, cast off 9 sts at beg of next row and foll alt row. *9 sts*

Work 1 row.

Bind off rem 9 sts.

With RS facing, slip center 26 sts onto a holder, rejoin yarn to rem sts, patt to end.

Complete to match first side, reversing all shapings.

SLEEVES

Using US 6 needles and yarn B, cast on 42(42:46:46) sts.

Work 20 rows in rib as given for left panel of Back and dec 2(0:2:0) sts evenly across last row. *40(42:44:46) sts*

Change to US 7 needles.

Cont in garter st and inc 1 st at each end of 5th row, then every foll 4th row until there are 66 sts, then every foll 6th row until there are 96(98:100:102) sts.

Cont straight in garter st until sleeve measures 21¼(21¼: 21⅝:21⅝)in, ending with a WS row.

Shape top

Bind off 5 sts at beg of next 2 rows. *86(88:90:92) sts*

Dec 1 st at each end of next row, then on 8 foll alt rows, then on every row until 36(38:40:42) sts rem.

Bind off 12 sts at beg of next 2 rows.

Bind off rem 12(14:16:18) sts.

COLLAR

Join right shoulder seam.

With RS facing, US 6 needles and yarn A, pick up and knit 15 sts down left front neck, knit across 26 sts on center front holder, pick up and knit 15 sts up right front neck, 4 sts down right back neck, knit across 34 sts on back neck holder, then pick up and knit 4 sts up left back neck. *98 sts*

Beg with row 2 of rib, work until collar measures 4⅜in.

Change to US 7 needles.

Cont in rib until collar measures 8¾in.

Bind off in rib.

FINISHING

Join left shoulder and collar seam, reversing seam on last 4⅜in of collar.

Turn collar onto RS of garment.

Sew right and left side panels to front and back cable panels.

Join side and sleeve seams.

Sew sleeves into armholes, easing to fit.

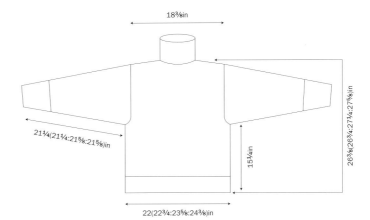

18⅜in

21¼(21¼:21⅝:21⅝)in

15¼in

26⅜(26¾:27¼:27⅝)in

22(22¾:23⅝:24⅜)in

Cable Slipover

SIZE

Extra small:small:medium:large

Bust 35¼:36¾:38⅜:40in

Length 21⅝:22:22⅜:22¾in

YARN

RYC Cotton Jeans in 1¾oz (50g)
balls (100% cotton), approx 82yd
(75m)

7(7:8:8) x Blue Jeans 366 (A)

Rowan Handknit Cotton in 1¾oz
(50g) balls (cotton), approx 93yd
(85m)

2 x Tope 253 (B)

NEEDLES

1 pair US 6 needles

1 pair US 7 needles

Cable needle

GAUGE

21 sts and 26 rows to 4in
over cable patt and 20 sts and
35 rows over garter st, both on US
7 needles

ABBREVIATIONS

C6F = slip next 3 sts onto cable
needle and hold at front of work,
K3, then K3 from cable needle.
See also page 142.

BACK

LEFT BACK PANEL

Using US 6 needles and yarn B,
cast on 14(14:18:18) sts.

Row 1 (RS): K2, * P2, K2, rep from
* to end.

Row 2: P2, * K2, P2, rep from *
to end.

These 2 rows form rib.

Work 18 more rows in rib and dec
4(2:4:2) sts evenly across last row.
10(12:14:16) sts

Change to US 7 needles.

Work straight in garter st until panel
measures 11⅜(11¾:12¼:12⅝)in,
ending with a WS row.

Shape armhole

Bind off 4(5:6:7) sts at beg of next
row. *6(7:8:9) sts*

Work 1 row.

Dec 1 st at armhole edge (beg) of
next row and 4(5:6:7) foll alt rows.
Fasten off rem st.

RIGHT BACK PANEL

Work as given for Left Back Panel,
reversing shapings and working
1 row more before armhole shaping.

CABLE PANEL

Using US 6 needles and yarn A,
cast on 74 sts.

Work 20 rows in rib as given for
Left Back Panel and dec 4 sts
evenly across last row. *70 sts*

Change to US 7 needles.

Row 1 (RS): K6, * P2, K6, rep from
* to end.

Row 2 and every foll alt row: * P6,

K2, rep from * to last 6 sts, K6.

Row 3: K6, * P2, C6F, P2, K6, rep
from * to end.

Row 5: As row 1.

Row 6: As row 2.

These 6 rows form cable patt. **

Cont in cable patt until panel
measures 21(21⅜:21¾:22¼)in,
ending with a WS row.

Shape shoulders and back neck

Next row (RS): Keeping patt correct,
cast off 5 sts, patt until there are
15 sts on right-hand needle, turn
and leave rem sts on a holder.

Work each side of neck separately.

Next row: Patt 2tog, patt to end.

14 sts

Next row: Bind off 6 sts, patt to last
2 sts, patt 2tog. *7 sts*

Next row: Patt 2tog, patt to end.

Bind off rem 6 sts.

With RS facing, slip 30 sts at
center onto a holder, rejoin yarn A
to rem sts and patt to end.

Complete to match first side,
reversing all shapings.

FRONT

Work left and right panels as given
for Back.

CABLE PANEL

Work as given for cable panel of
Back to **.

Cont straight in cable patt until
18 rows less have been worked
than on back to shoulder shaping.

Shape neck

Next row (RS): Patt 27, turn and

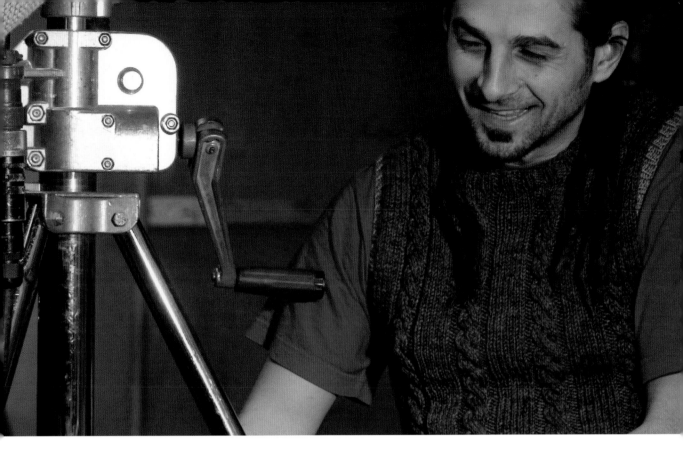

leave rem sts on a holder.

Work each side of neck separately.

Next row: Patt to end.

Dec 1 st at neck edge of next 5 rows, then at same edge on 5 foll alt rows. *17 sts*

Work 1 row.

Shape shoulder

Keeping patt correct, cast off 5 sts at beg of next row and 6 sts at beg of foll alt row. *6 sts*

Work 1 row.

Bind off rem 6 sts.

With RS facing, slip center 16 sts onto a holder, rejoin yarn to rem sts, patt to end.

Complete to match first side, reversing all shapings.

NECKBAND

Join right shoulder seam.

With RS facing, US 6 needles and yarn A, pick up and knit 20 sts down left front neck, knit across 16 sts on center front holder, pick up and knit 20 sts up right front neck, 4 sts down right back neck, knit across 30 sts back neck stitch holder then pick up and knit 4 sts up left back neck. *94 sts*

Beg with row 2 of rib, work 5 rows. Bind off in rib.

FINISHING

Sew right and left side panels to front and back cable panels.

Join left shoulder and neckband seam.

ARMHOLE EDGING

With RS facing, US 6 needles and yarn B, pick up and knit 81(85:89:93) sts evenly around armhole edge.

Row 1 (WS): P1, * K1, P1, rep from * to end.

Row 2: K1, * P1, K1, rep from * to end.

Rep rows 1 and 2 once more.

Bind off in rib.

Join side and armhole edging seams.

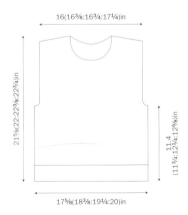

Cable Sweater

SIZE
Extra small:small:medium:large
Bust 40⅜:43¼:46⅜:49⅝in
Length 26⅜:26¾:27¼:27⅝in
Sleeve 20:20:20⅜:20⅜in

YARN
RYC Cotton Jeans in 1¾oz (50g)
balls (100% cotton), approx 82yd
(75m)

19(20:21:22) x Shingle 368 (A)
2 x Blue Jeans 366

NEEDLES
Pair of US 6 needles
Pair of US 7 needles
Cable needle

GAUGE
21 sts and 26 rows to 4in over
cable patt on US 7 needles

ABBREVIATIONS
C6F = slip next 3 sts onto cable
needle and hold at front of work,
K3, then K3 from cable needle.
See also page 142.

BACK
Using US 6 needles and yarn B,
cast on 114(122:130:138) sts.
Row 1 (RS): K2, * P2, K2, rep from
* to end.
Row 2: P2, * K2, P2, rep from *
to end.
These 2 rows form rib.
Work 22 more rows in rib and dec
6 sts evenly across last row.
108(116:124:132) sts
Change to US 7 needles and
yarn A.
1st and 3rd sizes only
Row 1 (RS): K1, * P2, K6, rep from
* to last 3 sts, P2, K1.
Row 2 and every foll alt row: P1, *
K2, P6, rep from * to last 3 sts,
K2, P1.
Row 3: K1, * P2, C6F, P2, K6,
rep from * to last 11 sts, P2, C6F,
P2, K1.
Row 5: As row 1.
Row 6: As row 2.
These 6 rows form cable patt.
2nd and 4th sizes only
Row 1, 2, 4, 5 and 6: As 1st and
3rd sizes.
Row 3: K1, * P2, C6F, P2, K6, rep
from * to last 3 sts, P2, K1.
These 6 rows form cable patt.
Cont in cable patt until back
measures 15⅜(15¾:16¼:16⅝)in,
ending with a WS row.
Place markers at each end of last
row for armholes. **
Cont straight in cable patt until
work measures 10in from markers,
ending with a WS row.

Shape shoulders and back neck
Next row (RS): Keeping patt correct,
bind off 14 sts, patt until there are
23(27:31:35) sts on right-hand
needle, turn and leave rem sts on
a holder.
Work each side of neck separately.
Next row: Patt 2tog, patt to end.
22(26:30:34) sts
Next row: Bind off 14 sts, patt
to last 2 sts, patt 2tog.
7(11:15:19) sts
Next row: Patt 2tog, patt to end.
Bind off rem 6(10:14:18) sts.
With RS facing, slip center 34 sts
onto a holder, rejoin yarn A to rem
sts and patt to end.
Complete to match first side,
reversing all shapings.

FRONT
Work as given for Back to **.
Cont straight in st st until 10 rows
less have been worked than on
Back to shoulder shaping.
Shape neck
Next row (RS): Patt 41(45:49:53),
turn and leave rem sts on a holder.
Work each side of neck separately.
Next row: Patt to end.
Dec 1 st at neck edge of next
7 rows. *34(38:42:46) sts*
Work 1 row.
Shape shoulder
Keeping patt correct, cast off
14 sts at beg of next and foll alt
row. *6(10:14:18) sts*
Work 1 row.
Bind off rem 6(10:14:18) sts.

With RS facing, slip center 26 sts onto a holder, rejoin yarn to rem sts, patt to end.

Complete to match first side, reversing all shapings.

SLEEVES

Using US 6 needles and yarn B, cast on 42(42:50:50) sts.

Work 24 rows in rib as given for Back and dec 4 sts evenly across last of these rows, ending with a WS row. *38(38:46:46) sts*

Change to US 7 needles and yarn A.

Row 1 (RS): Inc, K1, * P2, K6, rep from * to last 4 sts, P2, inc, K1. *40(40:48:48) sts*

Row 2: P3, * K2, P6, rep from * to last 5 sts, K2, P3.

Row 3: Inc, K2, * P2, C6F, P2, K6, rep from * to last 13 sts, P2, C6F, P2, K1, inc, K1. *42(42:50:50) sts*

Row 4: P4, * K2, P6, rep from * to last 6 sts, K2, P4.

Row 5: Inc, K3, * P2, K6, rep from * to last 6 sts, P2, K2, inc, K1. *44(44:52:52) sts*

Row 6: P5, * K2, P6, rep from * to last 7 sts, K2, P5.

These 6 rows form the cable panel and set the side incs.

Cont to inc as before, 1 st at

each end of next row and 3 foll alt rows, then every foll 4th row until there are 96(96:104:104) sts, working inc sts into cable patt where possible.

Cont straight in cable patt until sleeve measures 20(20:20⅜:20⅜)in, ending with a WS row.

Shape top

Keeping patt correct, dec 1 st at each end of next row, 3 foll alt rows, then on every row until 50(50:52:52) sts rem.

Bind off 13 sts at beg of next 2 rows.

Bind off rem 24(24:26:26) sts.

COLLAR

Join right shoulder seam.

With RS facing, US 6 needles and yarn B, pick up and knit 12 sts down left front neck, knit across 26 sts on center front holder, pick up and knit 12 sts up right front neck, 4 sts down right back neck, knit across 32 sts on back neck holder, then pick up and knit 4 sts up left back neck. *90 sts*

Beg with row 2 of rib, work until collar measures 4⅜in.

Change to US 7 needles.

Cont in rib until collar measures 8¾in.

Bind off in rib.

FINISHING

Join left shoulder and collar seam, reversing seam on last 4⅜in of collar.

Turn collar onto RS of garment.

Join side seams to markers.

Join sleeve seams.

Sew sleeves into armholes, easing to fit.

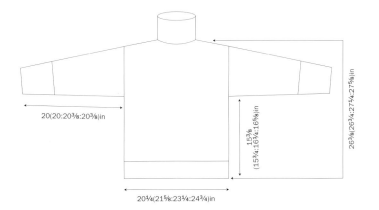

20(20:20⅜:20⅜)in

15⅜(15¾:16¼:16⅝)in

26⅜(26¾:27¼:27⅝)in

20¼(21⅝:23¼:24¾)in

Project Gallery

Spiderweb Bolero
Page 74

Lace and Ribbon Bolero
Page 78

Cap-sleeve Bolero
Page 80

Peacock Skirt
Page 82

Skating Skirt
Page 86

Puffball Skirt
Page 88

Tube Dress
Page 90

Seersucker Vest
Page 92

Peacock Dress
Page 94

Lurex Vest
Page 99

Project Gallery Continued

Chevron Waffle Cardigan
Page 102

Lace and Chevron Cardigan
Page 105

Tweed Cardigan
Page 108

Long Waistcoat
Page 111

Striped Tunic Dress
Page 114

Lurex Tunic
Page 116

Stocking Stitch Sweater
Page 118

Cable and Garter Sweater
Page 121

Cable Slipover
Page 124

Cable Sweater
Page 126

Starting Knitting

At Weardowney we get a lot of calls inquiring about knitting classes. Many are from novices to the craft of handknitting and we always tell them the same thing: "Once you can knit and purl, you can do anything." They don't always believe us, but after a class or two they are working away on their needles with confidence. In this section of the book, we put those classes down on paper so that you, too, can see how easy it is to start knitting.

Structured in an approachable way and illustrated with drawings that are as clear and accurate as they are beautiful, these techniques will open the door to the projects in this book.

Start by experimenting with holding the knitting needles. When you are knitting, the needle in the left hand has the stitches on it, so hold it from above, like a knife. The needle in the right hand can be held in the same way, or it can rest across the crook of your thumb, like a pen. As long as you can make stitches easily, hold the needles however you like.

You need to control the gauge of the yarn to create even stitches. Try running it over your right index finger, under the second finger, then over your ring finger. If this isn't keeping the yarn tight, then wrap it once around your little finger as well. As with holding the needles, it doesn't really matter how you gauge yarn, as long as your method works for you.

The left hand feeds the stitches towards the tip of its needle, while your right index finger moves the yarn back and forth to wrap it around the tip of the right-hand needle. At first the needles and yarn may feel awkward, but as you get better at knitting you will find it more and more comfortable.

You are ready to cast on, the first step in any knitting project. There are various different methods of casting on, but you only need to learn one to get started. Read the instructions and practice until you have cast on a lovely even row of 20 stitches.

Now you can move on to the knit stitch. You will discover that in casting on you have more or less learned this stitch—all you are doing is keeping it on the right-hand needle rather than putting it on the left-hand needle. Having conquered knit stitch, purl stitch will hold few mysteries, and now you are knitting. The rest is just variations on these two stitches.

CASTING ON

1 About 15cm from the end of the yarn, wind it twice around the first two fingers of your left hand, with the second loop behind the first one. Use the tip of a knitting needle to draw the second loop through the first one. Pull gently on the ends of the yarn to tighten the knot on the needle. This is the first cast on stitch.

2 Hold the needle with the knot in your left hand. From left to right, put the tip of the right-hand needle into the front of the knot. *Wind the ball end of the yarn around the tip of the right-hand needle, going under then across the top. Pull the loop of yarn around the tip of the right-hand needle through the slip knot.

Cable cast on

This cast on is known as a "cable cast on" or a "two-needle cast on." It produces a firm, even edge that blends in very well with the look of stockinette stitch.

If you are struggling to get an even row of cast on stitches, try putting your needle between the last two stitches before tightening the very last one. With the needle in place, pull gently on the yarn to tighten the stitch around the needle, then proceed to loop the yarn around the tip.

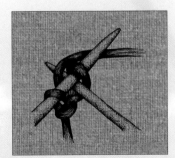

3 Slip the loop of yarn on the right-hand needle onto the left-hand needle and pull gently on the ball end of the yarn to tighten the stitch. You have cast on a second stitch.

4 For the next and all subsequent stitches, put the needle between the last two stitches, not through a stitch. Repeat from * until you have cast on all the stitches needed.

KNIT STITCH

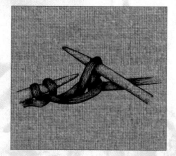

1 Hold the needle with the stitches on in your left hand. *From left to right, put the tip of the right-hand needle into the front of the first stitch. Wind the yarn around the tip of the right-hand needle, just as you did when casting on.

2 Pull the loop on the tip of the right-hand needle through the stitch on the left-hand needle. You now have a brand new stitch on the right-hand needle.

3 Keeping the new stitch on the right-hand needle, slip the first stitch off the left-hand needle. You have knitted one stitch. Repeat from * until you have knitted all the stitches. Then swap the needles in your hands and you are ready to begin again.

PURL STITCH

  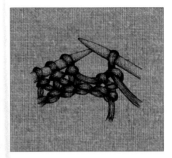

1 Hold the needle with the stitches on in your left hand. *From right to left, insert the tip of the right-hand needle into the front of the first stitch. From front to back, wind the working yarn over the tip of the right-hand needle.

2 Pull the loop on the tip of the right-hand needle through the stitch on the left-hand needle.

3 Keeping the new stitch on the right-hand needle, slip the first stitch off the left-hand needle. You have purled one stitch. Repeat from * until you have purled all the stitches. Then swap the needles in your hands and you are ready to begin again.

BINDING OFF

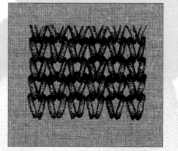

stockinette stitch

garter stitch

To bind off on a knit row, knit the first two stitches. * Use the tip of the left-hand needle to lift the first stitch over the second one and drop it off both needles. Knit another stitch. Repeat from * until you have cast off all the stitches. When you have just one stitch left on the right-hand needle, cut the yarn leaving a 15cm tail. Gently pull on the stitch to open it up a little, put the tail through the stitch and pull it tight. All of your stitches are safely cast off.

To bind off on a purl row, just purl the stitches instead of knitting them.

If you have cast on, worked alternate knit and purl rows, and cast off, you have worked stockinette stitch. On the front this fabric has rows of interlocking Vs. The back looks like lines of little scallops and is called reverse stockinette stitch.

If you have cast on, knitted a few rows, and bind off, you have worked garter stitch. This knitted fabric is reversible; both sides have rows of ridges. It is very elastic as the rows are quite compressed.

INCREASING

make one (M1)

1 Pick up the loop between the next two stitches by putting the tip of the right-hand needle through the front of the loop.

2 From the front, slip the picked-up loop onto the left-hand needle. Now knit into the back of it.

increase (inc)

Knit into the stitch in the usual way but do not drop the original stitch off the left-hand needle. Now knit into the back of the stitch and then drop the original stitch.

yarn over (yo)

Bring the yarn to the front between the needles. Take it back over the top of the right-hand needle. Now knit the next stitch in the usual way. On the next row, just knit or purl onto the loop created by the yarn over.

Open and closed

There are two types of increases, closed increases and open increases, and here you are learning both.

"Make one" and "increase" are both closed increases. That is to say, they do not leave a hole in the knitted fabric. "Make one" is almost invisible and all you can see of "increase" is a small bar of yarn across the front of the second stitch.

"Yarn over" is an open increase—it leaves a deliberate hole in the knitted fabric. This increase is used in knitting lace and eyelet patterns. It is often paired with "knit two together" (see page 140) to create a decorative hole, but keep the stitch count the same across the row.

DECREASING

knit two together (k2tog)

slip one, knit one, pass slipped stitch over (skpo)

This decrease involves knitting two stitches together to make one, and slants to the right on a knit row.

From left to right, put the tip of the right-hand needle through the front of the second stitch from the end of the left-hand needle, then through the first one. Knit the two stitches together as if they were one.

1 This method is similar to casting off, and slopes to the left on a knit row.

Put the tip of the right-hand needle into the next stitch as if to knit it, but just slip it off the left-hand needle; this is called slipping a stitch knitwise. Now knit the next stitch in the usual way.

2 Use the tip of the left-hand needle to lift the slipped stitch over the knitted one and drop it off both needles, as you did when you cast off a stitch.

CABLES

cable four back (C4B)

1 This cable is shown worked over four stitches, but it can be a different number. Cable back twists to the right.

Work to the position of the cable. Slip the next two stitches on the left-hand needle onto a cable needle and leave it at the back of the work.

2 Knit the next two stitches on the left-hand needle.

3 Now knit the two stitches on the cable needle.

cable four front (C4F)

Cable front twists to the left. Work a front cable in the same way as a back cable, but once you have slipped the two stitches onto the cable needle, leave the it at the front of the work instead of at the back.

SEWING UP   ABBREVIATIONS

Thread a knitter's sewing needle with a long length of the yarn you used to knit the project. Right-side up, lay the pieces to be joined next to one another. Start at the bottom edge of the piece on the right.

Working between the first and second stitches in from the edge, take the needle under the bars of two rows. Then take the needle under the corresponding two bars on the other piece of knitting. Go back to the first piece, put the needle in where it came out, and take it under the next two bars.

Continue in this way, zigzagging between the two pieces and taking the needle under two bars each time. Gently pull up the stitches to close the seam as you work.

When you have completed the seam, sew the ends of yarn into the back of the seam.

A, B, C	colors as indicated in the pattern	**psso**	pass slipped stitch over
alt	alternate	**rem**	remain, remaining
approx	approximate	**rep(s)**	repeat(s)
beg	begin, beginning, begins	**rev st st**	reverse stockinette stitch
C4B	cable four (or number stated) back	**RS**	right side
C4F	cable four (or number stated) forward	**skpo**	slip one, knit one, pass slipped stitch over
cont	continue	**sl**	slip
dec(s)	decrease, decreasing, decreases	**st(s)**	stitch(es)
in	inch(es)	**st st**	stockinette stitch
inc(s)	increase, increasing, increases	**tbl**	through the back of the loop
k2tog	knit two (or number stated) together	**tog**	together
K	knit	**WS**	wrong side
M1	make one stitch	**yd**	yard(s)
oz	ounce(s)	**yfwd**	yarn forward
p2sso	pass the 2 slipped stitches over the last stitch(es) knit	**yo**	yarn over
p2tog	purl two (or number stated) together	**yon**	yarn over needle
P	purl	*****	repeat instructions between/following * as many times as instructed
patt(s)	pattern(s)	**[ ]**	repeat instructions between [ ] as many times as instructed

Index

Bibliography

Madsen, Axel; *Chanel: A Woman of her Own;* Owl Books; 1991

Black, Sandy; *Knitwear in Fashion*, Thames and Hudson, 2002

Blackman, Cally; "Handknitting in Britain from 1908-39: the work of Marjory Tillotson"; *Textile History*; 177-200, 1998

Burnham, Dorothy, "Coptic knitting, an ancient technique", *Textile History*, vol.3, Dec, 1972

Blum, Dilys E.; *Shocking! The art and fashion of Elsa Schiaparelli*, Yale University press, New haven, 2003

Ewing, Elizabeth; *History of twentieth century fashion*; Batsford; 2001

Grass, Milton.N, "The origins of the art of knitting", *Archaeology*, VIII, Autumn 1955

McDermott, Catherine, *Made in Britain*; Octopus, 2002

McQuaid, Matilda; *Extreme Textiles: Designing for High Performance*, Princeton Architectural Press, 2005

M Hartley & J Ingilby, *The Old Hand-Knitters of the Dales* (1951), reprinted by the Dalesman, 1969

Harvey, M; *Patons: A Story of Handknitting* Patons & Baldwins Limited, 1985

de la Haye and Tobin; *Chanel, the Couturiere at work*; V&A publications, 1994

Hinchcliffe, F; *Knit One, Purl One - Historic and Contemporary Knitting the V&A's Collection* Victoria and Albert Museum, 1985

Howell, Georgina; *In Vogue, Sixty years of celebrities and fashion from British Vogue*, Penguin, 1975

Laver, James; *Costume and Fashion*, Thames and Hudson; 1996

Levey, S.M, "Illustrations of the History of Knitting Selected from the Collection of the Victoria and Albert Museum", *Textile History,* vol. 1, no 2, 1969

Menkes, Susie; *The Knitwear Revolution*, Bell & Hyman, 1983

Norbury, J; *The Knitter's Craft,* London, 1950

Norbury, J; *The Penguin Knitting Book*, Harmondsworth, 1957

Norbury, J; *Traditional Knitting Patterns*, London, 1962

Parkins, Wendy; 'Celebrity Knitting and the temporality of postmodernity', *Fashion Theory*, Vol 8, issue 4, 2004

Pearson, Michael, *Traditional Knitting*, Collins, London, 1984

Pearson, Michael, *Traditional Knitting of the British Isles, part 1 - Fisher Gansey Patterns of North East England*, Esteem Press, 1978

Rutt, Richard, *A History of hand-knitting*, Batsford, London, 1987

Sischy, Ingrid; *Time*; '100 most influential people of the twentieth century', June 8, 1998

Thomas, Mary; *Mary Thomas's Knitting Book* (1938) reprinted by Hodder & Stoughton, 1985

Thomas, Mary; *Mary Thomas's Book of Knitting Patterns*, (1943) reprinted by Hodder & Stoughton, 1985

Turnau I. and Ponting K.G., "Knitted Masterpieces", *Textile History*, vol.7, 1976

Turnau, I; *History of Knitting before Mass Production*, Warszawa, 1991

Wilcox, Claire; *Radical Fashion*, V&A publications, 2000

Wilcox, Claire; *Vivienne Westwood*; V&A publications, 2004

Fashion, The Collection of the Kyoto Costume Institute: A History from the 18th to the 20th Century, Taschen, 2002

Resources

Rowan Yarns c/o Westminster Fibers
165 Ledge Street
Nashua, NH 03063
www.westminsterfibers.com

Rowan Yarn Classic (RYC)
see Rowan Yarns
www.ryclassic.com

Twilleys of Stamford
www.herschners.com

The publishers would like to thank the following companies for lending clothes for photography:

Spider Web Bolero: unitard, American Apparel.

Lace and Ribbon Bolero: leggings, American Apparel.

Peacock Skirt: leggings, American Apparel; ballet shoes, Dancia.

Skating Skirt and Cap-sleeve Bolero: polo neck body, Wolford; leggings, American Apparel.

Puffball Skirt: white ruffle blouse, Berube; tights, Jonathan Aston; ballet shoes, Dancia.

Tube Dress: tights, Jonathan Aston; necklace, Loulou de la Falaise.

Seersucker Tank Top: trousers and shoes, Louis Vuitton; bow tie, stylist's own.

Peacock Dress: polo neck body, Wolford; leggings, American Apparel; shoes, Celine.

Lurex Tank Top: jacket, Louis Vuitton.

Chevron Waffle Cardigan: grey all-in-one, Metallicus; tights, Jonathan Aston; ballet shoes, Dancia.

Lace and Chevron Cardigan: tights, Jonathan Aston; ballet shoes, Dancia.

Long Vest: leggings, American Apparel; ballet shoes, Dancia.

Striped Tunic Dress: leggings American Apparel; bowler hat, stylist's own.

Lurex Tunic: tights, Jonathan Aston.

Berube: 020 7729 3147 for stores
Dancia: www.dancia.com for stores
Metalicus: www.metalicus.com for stores
American Apparel: www.americanapparel.com for stores
Loulou de la Falaise: 020 7725 9694 for stores
Louis Vuitton: www.louisvuitton.com for stores
Wolford: www.wolford.com for stores
Celine: www.celine.com for stores